Contents

Preface *vii*

1 Introduction and Overview *1*

2 The Participation Rate Differentials: Evidence and Review *7*

3 Racial Differences in the Discouraged Worker Effect *41*

4 The Discouraged Worker Effect in a Dynamic Model of Labor Supply *63*

5 Parameter Estimates from the Seattle Income Maintenance Experiments *83*

6 Sources of Trends in Participation: Further Evidence from the Gross Flows *99*

7 Conclusions and Suggestions for Further Research *111*

Notes *113*

Bibliography *117*

Index *123*

AUDREY COHEN COLLEGE
50664000079337
Williams, Donald R./Labor force partici
HD6273 .W48 1987 C.1 STACKS 1987

COLLEGE FOR HUMAN SERVICES
LIBRARY
345 HUDSON STREET
NEW YORK, N.Y. 10014

Labor Force Participation of Black and White Youth

by
Donald R. Williams

UMI Research Press
Ann Arbor, Michigan

Copyright © 1987, 1984
Donald R. Williams
All rights reserved

Produced and distributed by
UMI Research Press
an imprint of
University Microfilms, Inc.
Ann Arbor, Michigan 48106

Library of Congress Cataloging in Publication Data

Williams, Donald R., 1956-
  Labor force participation of black and white youth.

  (Research in business economics and public policy ;
no. 11)
  Revision of thesis (Ph.D.)—Northwestern University,
1984.
  Bibliography: p.
  Includes index.
  1. Youth—Employment—United States. 2. Afro-American
youth—Employment. I. Title. II. Series.
HD6273.W48   1987   331.3'412'0973   87-5868
ISBN 0-8357-1804-2 (alk. paper)

Preface

The employment difficulties of black youth are well known (the black teenage unemployment rate is invariably mentioned in news reports at the beginning of each month) and unusually persistent. My first attempt at examining this serious social problem was to try to answer the question: To what extent is a high black teenage unemployment rate the result of labor market discrimination? In the course of that work it became clear that one major contributor to black teenage unemployment was their lack (relative to white teenagers) of "labor market experience," due in part to their not being able to find jobs when they looked, but also due to the fact that they were much less likely to look, as measured by the labor force participation rate. Yet in the studies of youth labor markets over the past decades, social scientists have concentrated primarily on the unemployment rate and have paid little, explicit attention to labor force participation. This book attempts to fill that void.

Since completion of my earlier studies in this area I have benefited greatly from correspondence with Professors Harry Holzer and Randall Olsen, and I would like to thank them for their interest. I am also grateful to the Kent State University Office of Research and Sponsored Programs for its support.

1

Introduction and Overview

The purpose of this study is to document and attempt to explain the differences in the labor force participation behavior of black and white male teenagers. Black teens are less likely than whites are to participate in the labor force, their participation has been declining, and it fluctuates widely over the course of the business cycle. Yet this is the only study to date which sets out to explain this behavior. In attempting to do so, the primary focus is on the relationship between labor force participation behavior and employment opportunities. It is argued that the racial differences in participation are primarily the result of racial differences in employment opportunities and changes in those opportunities over time, rather than racial differences in "behavior," or preferences for work. To the extent that this is true, there remains a role for government assistance in the elimination of this important racial differential, through jobs programs targeted at minority youth, through anti-discrimination policies, or indeed through the management of aggregate demand. The results of the empirical analyses presented here indicate that the argument has validity, which suggests the need for an active governmental response.

As noted above, the differences take three forms. First, black youth are less likely to participate in the labor force than are white youth. In December of 1985, the labor force participation rate for black males aged 16–19 years was 45.6 percent (seasonally adjusted), compared to 58.5 percent for whites. As a consequence of this difference, black youth accumulate less information about the labor market than do white youth and they accumulate fewer skills for use on-the-job. This lack of labor market participation among black teenagers places many black youth at a relative disadvantage when they become young adults.

The second racial difference lies in recent trends in participation, such that the difference between black and white participation rates is getting even larger. This is particularly true for the decade of the seventies. In December of 1972 (the first year that the U.S. Department of Labor published adjusted statistics by race), the seasonally adjusted participation rates were 48 and 60.9 percent for black and white teens, respectively. In December of 1979, the rate for blacks was 40.3 percent, compared to 65.9 percent for whites. The participation rate for black teens therefore fell considerably, while for white teens it actually increased. Not only have black youth been disadvantaged because of a lack of participation, but the problem has been getting worse. In addition to differences in the levels and trends in labor force participation, a racial difference also exists in the behavior of the participation rate over the business cycle. When we enter a recession and aggregate demand and employment opportunities decrease, the participation rate decreases more for blacks than for whites. The relative impact in terms of the loss of human capital and labor market skills associated with economic downturns is therefore greater for blacks than for whites and, again, the result is that black youth are relatively less attractive to employers than are white youth. Each of these racial differences in participation contributes to the black youth "employment problem" in general, and each therefore is an obstacle to racial economic equality.

There are many possible causes of these differences. Standard economic models of labor supply would suggest that some workers may have lower levels of participation than others because they place a higher value on time spent in nonmarket activities (thought to be a function of tastes, family responsibilities, nonlabor income, and ambition), because they face higher costs of search, because they have lower wages, or because they have fewer employment opportunities. If black and white teenagers differ with respect to some of these variables, then they will exhibit differential participation rates as a result. Black and white participation rates may be diverging simply because racial differences in these variables may be getting larger. Likewise, racial differences in cyclic variations in these variables may contribute to the cyclic differences in participation.

I argue, however, that most of the reasons listed above for racial differences in *levels* of participation do little to explain the differences in trend or cyclic rate of change. For example, the wages of teenaged black males have increased relative to whites over the past decade, not decreased. And because recent work indicates that black teens are at least as willing to work as whites and seem to have as much of a "work ethic," we cannot conclude that the value of leisure has been rising for blacks relative to whites over the past decade. It also is difficult to conclude that the value of leisure rises more (or falls by less) for blacks in an economic downturn than it does for whites. Indeed, the opposite should be true if blacks are more likely to have other family members become unemployed as aggregate demand declines. The one explanation that is an important contributor to all the racial differences in participation is the notion that there exist racial differences in the behavior of employment opportunities. As I have noted, labor supply models generally predict that participation is positively related to employment opportunities (in the context of economic downturns this is the well known "discouraged worker effect"). Racial differences in participation behavior can clearly be seen as the result of the fact that black male teenagers face fewer employment opportunities than do white teens, the opportunities for blacks are declining relative to whites over time, and they are more sensitive to cyclic forces than are the opportunities for whites. Of course an alternative hypothesis might be that the employment opportunities faced by blacks and whites indeed behave in the same ways, and racial differences in participation rate behavior are instead the result of racial differences in the *response* to levels, trends, or cyclic changes in employment opportunities. One important goal of this study is to differentiate between these hypotheses. Nevertheless, understanding the relationship between participation rates and employment opportunities is an important step toward understanding the racial differentials in participation.

The results of the analyses presented here provide many insights into these relationships, both theoretical and empirical. A maintained hypothesis of the study is that in order to best understand the determinants of levels or changes in participation rates we need to identify the determinants of the flows between nonparticipation and participation that generate them. This is done by concentrating on the determinants of the probability of moving from one labor market state to another, called "flow probabilties." Changes in the levels of these probabilities are the sources of changes in the labor force participation rate. I use a model of labor market flows in this study which allows us to examine explicitly the relationships between transition probabilities, worker characteristics, and the level of aggregate demand. A very appealing aspect of the model is its characterization of transitions between states of the world as being jointly determined by the arrival of some events (for example, job offers) and individuals' choices whether or not to change their state (e.g., whether to accept the offers). We can therefore examine the relationship between the level of aggregate demand and the rate at which people make labor market transitions both in terms of the effect aggregate demand has on the arrival of job offers and the effect aggregate demand has on the individuals' optimal choices.

The results of an empirical analysis which attempts to distinguish between these effects suggest that racial differences in the relationship between employment opportunities and participation are indeed at least partially the result of racial differences in the effects of aggregate demand on job offers for workers out-of-the-labor-force, and on layoffs or firings for those who are employed. Further, the results indicate that decreases in employment opportunities cause black youth to increase, rather than decrease, their preference for employment over other states. The opposite is true for whites. On the other hand, the results also suggest that income transfer payments such as Aid to Families with Dependent Children (AFDC) affect workers' labor force participation through their "optimal choices," and these effects are stronger for blacks than for whites. As noted, the results are mixed, as we should probably expect. They do not show conclusively that racial differences in participation are solely the result of differences in opportunities. But nor do they suggest that differences in opportunities are not an important factor.

4   Introduction and Overview

The study is outlined as follows: Evidence of racial differences in levels, trends, and the volatility or cyclic rate of change of participation rates for male teenagers is presented in chapter 2. Based on published, monthly data from the U.S. Bureau of Labor Statistics for the 1972–85 time period, the analysis finds that blacks' participation rates are significantly lower and more volatile than are whites', and that they have exhibited a significant downward trend over that time period, while whites' rates have risen. I then discuss a number of hypotheses in explanation of these differences, including the notions that blacks face higher costs of search than whites, can expect lower wages, or place a higher value on leisure time.

Drawing from the existing literature and from government data sources, I point out that most of the "conventional" notions regarding differences between black and white male youth do little to explain even racial differences in levels of participation, much less trends or cyclical variations.

Chapter 3 presents the initial evidence that one source of racial differences in participation behavior lies in the relationship between participation and aggregate demand. Again using aggregate time series data for labor force participation rates and unemployment rates for the 1972–85 period, it is found that black male youth differ from whites in their participation responses to changes in their own unemployment rates by a factor of 2 to 1, with black youth exhibiting the stronger response. This is seen to be true also after accounting for possible differences in the lag structure of the response. These results are taken as an indication that black and white youth exhibit differential "discouraged worker effects," and they are discussed in that context.

It is also pointed out, however, that the level of labor force participation can fall as employment opportunities decline because an increased number of unemployed workers leave the labor force, because fewer workers enter the labor force, or because of a combination of the two. The analysis of the aggregate participation rate data does not allow identification of any racial differences in the responses of these flows. Data from the Current Population Survey "Gross Change Tabulations" does allow such an analysis. Using CPS monthly flows for the 1972–81 time period, I also present in chapter 3 a time-series regression analysis of the relationship between flow probabilities and the level of aggregate demand, as measured by both the prime-aged (25–54) male unemployment rate and, again, the youths' own race-specific rates. The results suggest that racial differences do exist in the responsiveness of these flows, particularly for transitions from unemployment to out-of-the-labor-force, from out-of-the-labor-force to unemployment, and from out-of-the-labor-force to employment. All of the racial differences in these flow probabilities are seen to contribute to the racial differential in the discouraged worker effect.

In chapter 4 I present the model of labor market dynamics described above. The model is presented in the context of the differential discouraged worker effect, with the particular goal of answering the following question: Is it possible for blacks to exhibit a stronger discouraged worker response as a result of factors other than differences in tastes? The model suggests that, in addition to differences in tastes, sources of the differential response can include differences in search costs, wage levels, and even the relative levels (rather than the rates of change) of employment opportunities. Once again the importance of racial differences in employment opportunities is stressed.

Chapter 5 presents estimates of the parameters of the model, using longitudinal data for black and white male teens from the Seattle Income Maintenance Experiments. I present reduced form estimates of the effects of the local unemployment rate on transition probabilities, after accounting for the effects of individual variations in age, years of schooling, expected wages, AFDC payments, and other public transfer payments. The results are similar to those in chapter 3, indicating that increases in the unemployment rate lead to increases in transitions from employment to unemployment and from nonparticipation to unemployment, and decreases in transitions from unemployment or nonparticipation to employment. Racial differences in the effects on the nonparticipation to employment and the employment to nonparticipation transition probabilities stand out as important contributors to differential participation behavior. I then present "structural" parameter estimates, which indicate, as noted above, that some of the racial differences should be attributed to differences in opportunities rather than differences in behavior.

Chapter 6 provides an analysis of the *trends* in labor force participation, again using the Gross Change data from the Current Population Survey. First, I identify the trends in transition rates over the past decade that have generated the trends in participation, and assess their importance. The results indicate that the widening gap in black and white participation rates can be attributed in large part to racial differences in trends in the unemployment to out-of-the-labor-force, out-of-the-labor-force to employment, employment to unemployment, and employment to out-of-the-labor-force transition probabilities. I estimate that elimination of these racial differences in trends would have reduced the racial participation rate differential by at least 25 percent. The most important difference seems to be the more drastic decline in the out-of-the-labor-force to employment transition probability exhibited by blacks. Elimination of that differential alone would have decreased the racial participation rate differential by more than 8 percent. Second, I estimate the contributions to these transition rate trends made by a number of exogenous variables, including the labor market activity of women, the minimum wage, and income transfers (such as AFDC payments), in addition to the level of aggregate demand. The analysis indicates that many of these factors have made significant contributions to the trends. The increased labor supply of women over the decade seems to have been particularly important in the decline in labor force activity exhibited by young black males. Because the response is probably not due to a wealth effect, the results suggest that the effect is felt primarily through competition from women for employment opportunities. Because the effect is race specific, it may signify the important role that employment discrimination plays in explaining race differences in participation.

I conclude in chapter 7 that, although the analysis in this study provides many insights into racial differences in participation, there is a great need for further research. The application of the methods of analysis developed here to other data sources, particularly the National Longitudinal Survey Youth Cohort, could lead to very important contributions. Even so, the main conclusion provided here, that racial differences in employment opportunities and their variation over time are primary causes of the fact that black youth participate so little in the labor market, is very important and must be kept in mind by policy makers when evaluating and attempting to eliminate racial economic inequality.

2

The Participation Rate Differentials: Evidence and Review

The evidence that black and white male teenagers have differed in the levels, trends, and volatility of their labor force participation rates over the past decade is presented in this chapter. I also present a survey of the many explanations for these differences that are found in the existing social science literature, including differences in school enrollment rates, military enlistment rates, family responsibilities, costs of search, the work ethic, and the advent of "black power." I argue that the root of racial differences in participation lies primarily in racial differences in employment opportunities, however, and so also discuss the reasons that they exist.

The Participation Rate Differentials

Since at least the mid-1950s, black male youth aged 16–19 have tended to participate in the labor force less than their white counterparts.[1] The decade of the seventies proved no exception to the rule, as can be seen in figure 2.1, where I present the annual average labor force participation rates for the 1972–85 time period. The average of the labor force participation rates for black youth over the entire 1972–85 time period was almost 19 percentage points less than the participation rate for white youth (43.4 vs. 62.2), a differential of more than 30 percent. The null hypothesis that the two rates are the same would be rejected at any conventional level of confidence.

As is easily seen from the figure, the gap is not only large, it is growing as well. While the participation rate for white youth has on average risen over the past decade, the participation rate for blacks has fallen, the continuation of a trend that dates back at least to 1954 (see Newman, 1979). The magnitudes of the trends in the most recent time period are indicated by the coefficients from a simple linear regression of the monthly participation rate on a "time" variable and time squared (to account for the nonlinearity apparent in the figure). These estimates are presented in tables 2.1 and 2.2, for both level and semilog specifications. The coefficient on the TIME variable in the semilog specification represents the monthly rate of change

8   *The Participation Rate Differentials*

Figure 2.1. Black and White Male Labor Force Participation Rates, 1972–85

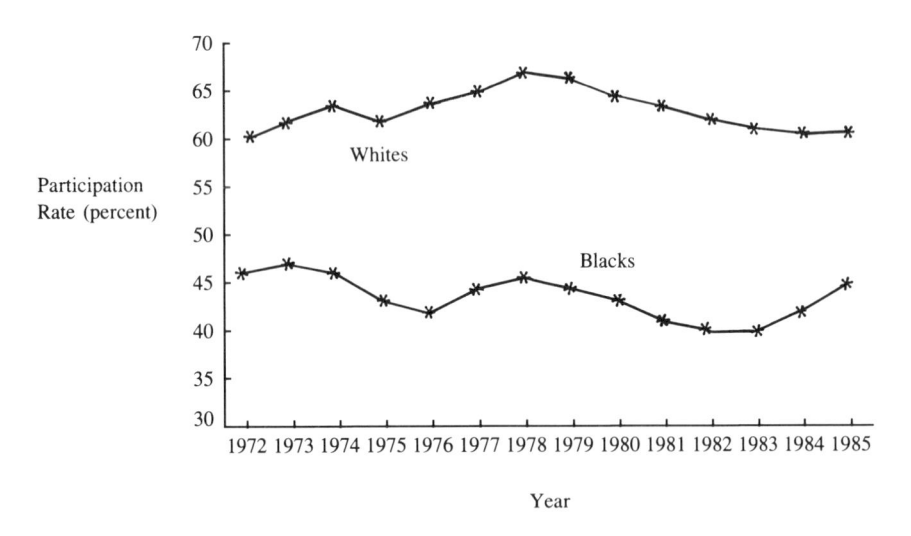

in the participation rate, in percentage terms. The equations are estimated separately, by race. I adjust for serial correlation of the residuals by using the Cochrane-Orcutt iterative technique, assuming a first-order autoregressive process. The data used are the monthly, seasonally adjusted civilian labor force participation rates for the two racial groups for the January 1972 to December 1985 period, as published by the Bureau of Labor Statistics (U.S. Department of Labor, 1983, 1986). The results in tables 2.1 and 2.2 indicate that the participation rate for blacks exhibited a significant downward trend over the sample time period, at a rate of nearly 1 percentage point per year. The participation rate for whites is estimated to have shown an increasing trend over the sample time period, though the rate of growth was declining, as is evidenced by the negative coefficient on the TIME2 variable. Indeed, the trend becomes negative after 1978, though the rate of decline is not nearly as great as it is for blacks.

Because it is not apparent in the annual data in figure 2.1, I should note that the participation rate data jumps significantly, from 37.2 to 49 percent for blacks, between April and August of 1977. This is probably the effect of the Youth Employment and Demonstration Projects Act (YEDPA) of the Carter administration. The act created hundreds of thousands of jobs (targeted at inner-city youth) for the summer of 1977. The results of a regression analysis designed to account for the YEDPA program's effects are presented in table 2.3. Three regression equation specifications are used. In the first, a simple dummy variable which takes the value 1 for all months after and including June 1977 (YEDPA1), is added to the equation estimated above. In the second, the data is fitted to a broken time trend, where a

Table 2.1. Time Trend Estimates
Dependent Variable = Monthly Labor Force
Participation Rate, 1972–85

Independent Variable	Coefficient (*t*-Statistic) Blacks	Coefficient (*t*-Statistic) Whites
CONSTANT	48.4913*** (36.715)	59.8128*** (74.996)
TIME	−0.1146*** (−3.259)	0.1047*** (4.977)
TIME2	0.0005*** (2.463)	−0.0007*** (−6.030)
R^2	.104	.233
F	9.494	24.851
D.W.	2.194	2.398

*** Significant at a 99 percent level of confidence or greater.
** Significant at a 95 percent level of confidence or greater.
* Significant at a 90 percent level of confidence or greater.

Table 2.2. Time Trend Estimates
Dependent Variable = Log of Monthly Labor Force
Participation Rate, 1972–85

Independent Variable	Coefficient (*t*-Statistic) Blacks	Coefficient (*t*-Statistic) Whites
CONSTANT	3.8840*** (123.517)	4.0916*** (322.488)
TIME	−0.0026*** (−3.124)	0.0017*** (5.035)
TIME2	0.00001** (2.369)	−0.00001*** (−6.115)
R^2	.095	.239
F	8.643	25.745
D.W.	2.192	2.389

*** Significant at a 99 percent level of confidence or greater.
** Significant at a 95 percent level of confidence or greater.
* Significant at a 90 percent level of confidence or greater.

Table 2.3. Time Trend Estimates with YEDPA Variables
Dependent Variable=Monthly Labor Force Participation Rate, 1972–85

Independent Variable	Blacks (1)	Blacks (2)	Blacks (3)	Blacks (4)	Whites (5)	Whites (6)
CONSTANT	50.5214*** (45.310)	50.2570*** (41.901)	50.5402*** (48.944)	60.5010*** (80.541)	60.3526*** (76.119)	60.5356*** (93.046)
TIME	-0.2108*** (-5.948)	-0.1831*** (-5.208)	-0.2483*** (-6.584)	0.0738*** (3.204)	0.0845*** (3.723)	0.0475** (2.074)
TIME2	0.0008*** (4.690)	0.0004*** (2.517)	0.0016*** (3.770)	0.0006*** (-5.449)	-0.0007*** (-6.743)	-0.0000 (-0.113)
YEDPA1	5.2777*** (4.287)		16.5273*** (3.022)	1.6049** (2.191)		9.3731*** (2.795)
YEDPA2		0.0663*** (3.550)	-0.1633** (-2.100)		0.0182* (1.665)	-0.1122** (-2.329)
R^2	.237	.198	.280	.305	.277	.382
F	16.791	13.365	15.524	23.646	20.687	24.745
D.W.	2.161	2.178	2.141	2.328	2.349	2.272

*** Significant at a 99 percent level of confidence or greater.
** Significant at a 95 percent level of confidence or greater.
* Significant at a 90 percent level of confidence or greater.

new trend (YEDPA2) begins in June of 1977 (YEDPA2=YEDPA1*TIME). The third specification includes both YEDPA1 and YEDPA2. The results indicate that the program increased the participation rates for both groups, though the effect is largest for blacks. More important, though, note that the significant downward trend for blacks remains, even after the jump.

As noted, the effect of the racial difference in trends has been to widen the gap between black and white labor force participation rates, in both absolute and relative terms. In table 2.4, I present the results of estimating the parameters of a regression of the ratio of the white to black participation rate on TIME and TIME squared, in both "levels" and "logs" specifications. The results suggest a significant, secular growth in the relative racial differential.

The last observation one may have noted from figure 2.1 is that blacks and whites differ also in the degree of *volatility* of their participation rates. This is evidenced by the fact that the standard deviation for the monthly participation rate for blacks over the 1972–85 time period is more than 1-1/2 times the standard deviation for whites. This could simply be due to the differential slopes of the trends, however. A better measure of volatility might be the standard deviation of the *percent deviation from trend* of the participation rates for the two groups, using the data above and the trend estimates presented in table 2.1. These measures are shown in table 2.5. Also presented in the table are the estimates for the "pre-YEDPA" and "post-YEDPA" sample time periods. The entries in the ninth row of the table confirm the hypothesis that the participation rate for blacks is more

Table 2.4. Time Trend Estimates
Dependent Variable=Ratio of White to Black LFPR's, 1972–85

Independent Variable	Coefficient (*t*-Statistic) Levels	Coefficient (*t*-Statistic) Logs
CONSTANT	1.2288*** (37.051)	0.2114*** (9.398)
TIME	0.0059*** (6.675)	0.0042*** (6.996)
TIME2	−0.00003*** (−6.225)	−0.00002*** (−6.500)
R^2	.218	.235
F	22.815	25.167
D.W.	2.089	2.100

*** Significant at a 99 percent level of confidence or greater.
 ** Significant at a 95 percent level of confidence or greater.
  * Significant at a 90 percent level of confidence or greater.

12 The Participation Rate Differentials

Table 2.5. Descriptive Statistics: Deviations from Trend in Black and White Labor Force Participation Rates, 1972–85

	Standard Deviation	
	Blacks	**Whites**
Raw Data	3.169	2.156
Pre-YEDPA	3.550	1.312
Post-YEDPA	2.689	2.555
Detrended Data	2.129	0.973
Pre-YEDPA	2.516	0.847
Post-YEDPA	1.828	1.044
Percent Deviation from Trend Data	4.891	1.576
Pre-YEDPA	5.660	1.370
Post-YEDPA	4.305	1.693

Note: These estimates are for monthly, seasonally adjusted LFPR's. The "detrended data" were computed using the specifications in table 2.1.

volatile than that for whites: the black standard deviation is more than 3 times the standard deviation for the whites. The reasons for this difference will be seen to be of primary concern in the chapters to come.

The pre- and post-YEDPA comparisons indicate that in the latter portion of the decade (post-YEDPA), the black rate is relatively less volatile than in the earlier period. One explanation for this phenomenon is that the YEDPA program increased blacks' employment enough that the participation rate effects of future changes in the level of aggregate demand were dampened, since employed workers are less likely to drop out of the labor force over the business cycle than are unemployed workers, as will be discussed. In sum, the evidence from the 1970s and early 1980s indicates that black and white male youth differ in their labor force participation rates in a number of ways: black youth's participation levels are significantly lower, they exhibit diverging trends, and the blacks rates are more variable over time. The reasons for these differences follow.

Explanations

Many of the factors that work to determine the level of labor force participation at a point in time also affect changes in the level over time, and so are determinants of the trends and cyclic changes noted. For instance, suppose that the participation rate varies inversely with the costs of search associated with unemployment. Then if the costs of search have risen over time we should expect participation rates to have fallen. Likewise, if costs of search vary cyclically, then we would expect participation rates to exhibit cyclic behavior, also.

In addition, variables can affect the participation rate over time in less direct ways. Suppose we can write the participation rate, r, as a function of some variable, Z, that depends on time: $r(t) = R(Z(t))$. Then r will change with time in response to changes in Z, since

$$\frac{\delta r}{\delta t} = \frac{\delta R}{Z} \cdot \frac{\delta Z}{\delta t}$$

is not equal to zero as long as Z has some effect on r. Clearly, observed changes in r depend on $\delta R/\delta Z$. It is possible, of course, that $\delta R/\delta Z$ depends on the level of Z (the effect of Z on r is nonlinear). Further, $\delta R/\delta Z$ may depend on a number of other variables (characteristics of the workers, for instance) that do not vary over time at all. The response which r exhibits to a change in Z may depend on the level of schooling of the workers, for instance, or whether the workers are married or single. In sum, variables that affect participation rate levels can contribute to participation rate trends or cyclic changes through their own trend or cyclic components, and also through their levels, due to nonlinearities and interactions with other variables. Consequently, *racial differences* in levels, trends, and cyclic changes in participation can be seen to be the result of racial differences in both changes and levels of workers' characteristics and economic environments. In other words, racial differences in $\delta R/\delta Z$ can be due to racial differences in $\delta Z/\delta t$ or in $\delta R/\delta Z$, which may be attributed to race alone or differences in worker characteristics other than race.

A number of hypotheses regarding the exact relationships between Z, r, and other variables stem from the models of labor force participation behavior developed in the economics literature. I will discuss these relationships in detail in this section. Certainly, some variables affect participation rates only through their effects on other variables. For example, the minimum wage may affect the probability that a worker will be able to find a job if he searches, but there may be no reason why it should affect the participation decision directly. To the extent that job availability affects the participation decision, the minimum wage will affect participation, but only indirectly.[2] The set of such variables, having only indirect effects on participation, will be discussed below but only in the context of their effects on employment opportunities. I begin with a discussion of the variables that directly affect participation.

Sources of Differences in Participation Rate Behavior

The now standard static analysis of the labor supply or hours of work decision made popular by Lewis (1957), Mincer (1962), Becker (1965), and Cain (1966) predicts that whether a worker is a labor force participant or not depends critically on the worker's tastes (which determine the relative utilities of consumption goods and leisure), wealth, and expected wage if employed.[3] Holding tastes constant, more wealthy people (assuming leisure is a normal good), and high-wage workers will tend to participate more than low-wage workers. These results refer to workers who are making the decision to work at some offered wage, or not to participate in the market at all. The recognition of "unemployment" as a state distinct from employment and out-of-the-labor-force implies that costs of search also enter the participation decision.

This can be seen clearly in the context of a simple "dynamic" model of labor force participation, where a worker is defined to be a participant if he works or if he looks for work. Suppose individuals derive utility from leisure and income received from work, and that they place a value of u on the utility they derive from leisure and w on the utility they derive from income. If an individual does not participate in the labor force he therefore receives u. If he participates and works, he receives w. If he participates but does not work (he is unemployed), then suppose he receives $u-c$, where c is the cost (in terms of the value of leisure) associated with searching for work. Let p be the probability that he finds a job, given that he participates. He therefore will participate only if

$$(1-p)(u-c) + p \cdot w > u.$$

This equation implies that the probability a worker participates varies directly with w and p, and varies inversely with u and c.[4] Factors that tend to increase u or c, such as a greater preference for leisure or more nonlabor income from accumulated wealth or government transfer payments, will therefore decrease one's propensity to participate in the labor force. Likewise, factors that increase w or p (or what is sometimes called the "expected wage," $w \cdot p$) will increase one's propensity to participate. We should therefore look to differences across workers in tastes, wealth, expected income, and costs of search as sources of differences across workers in participation. When discussing the determinants of differences in participation behavior we must keep in mind that we want to explain differences in all its aspects: levels, trends, and volatility. Some factors that serve to explain the fact that blacks participate less than whites do nothing to explain the fact that the difference is growing. I will attempt to simultaneously discuss the sources of the different aspects of participation behavior.

Some analyses of racial differences in participation and employment fail to do so, however. These concern the hypotheses that participation rate differences are explained by differential school and military enrollment rates. The analyses do little to explain *why* these differentials exist. But they have bearing on this subject, nonetheless.

Differences in School Enrollment

One often-cited reason for the divergent trends in black and white youth participation is that black youth have increased their school enrollment rates relative to whites, in response, say, to increased returns to education. Since school and work are substitutes, so the argument goes, as blacks' enrollment rates increase then blacks must therefore decrease their labor force participation by more than whites.[5] It is true that black and white school enrollment rates have converged in the post-war period, and in fact that blacks' enrollment rates surpassed those of whites in the 1970s, especially for the 20- to 24-year-old age group. The difference is not great for the younger age groups, however, as is evidenced in table 2.6. In 1984, the school enrollment rate for black 16- and 17-year olds (of both sexes) was 92.5 percent, compared to 91.2 percent for whites. The enrollment rates for 18- and 19-year olds are much lower, but for both races. The rates in 1984 were 44.2 and 51.1 percent for blacks and whites, respectively. The table also suggests that the convergence in rates cited above occurred before 1972. The school enrollment hypothesis therefore does little to explain the divergence in the participation rate data since 1972. It also certainly does not explain the racial difference in *levels* of participation. Table 2.7 tells a slightly different story: blacks may enroll in school as much as whites, but those that are in school are much less likely to participate in the labor market than whites that are in school. Though the data includes 20- and 21-year olds, it is probably safe to conclude that the 16- to 19-year-old blacks that are in school participate in work much less than their white counterparts. The degree to which this is true in a given year seems to depend on the level of aggregate demand, though (compare 1981

Table 2.6. School Enrollment Rates among Teenage Males, 1972–84
(Figures from October of Each Year)

	16–17-Year-Olds			18–19-Year-Olds		
	% Enrolled		Blacks as a	% Enrolled		Blacks as a
Year	Whites	Blacks	% of Whites	Whites	Blacks	% of Whites
1972	90.4	88.9	98.3	51.5	47.7	92.6
1973	89.4	89.0	99.6	48.4	43.5	89.9
1974	88.2	90.1	102.2	45.5	46.1	101.3
1975	91.0	88.2	96.9	49.6	49.9	100.6
1976	90.6	90.9	100.3	46.9	54.9	117.1
1977	89.5	92.5	103.4	47.7	50.5	105.9
1978	88.9	92.8	104.4	47.2	50.5	107.0
1979	90.3	94.6	104.8	46.1	48.0	104.1
1980	88.8	90.8	102.3	47.5	42.8	90.1
1981	90.5	92.1	101.8	49.2	51.9	105.5
1982	91.0	92.2	101.3	48.5	46.5	95.5
1983	91.6	91.8	100.2	50.7	46.6	91.9
1984*	91.2	92.5	101.4	51.1	44.2	86.5

*The data for this year is for both males and females.

Source: 1972–79: U.S. Department of Labor, *Employment and Earnings*, various issues; 1980–83: Bureau of the Census, *Current Population Reports*, Series P20, various issues; 1984: *Statistical Abstract of the United States*, 1986.

16 *The Participation Rate Differentials*

Table 2.7. Labor Force Participation Rates of Students*
by Race, 16–21 Years Old, 1972–84
(Figures from March of Each Year)
(Percent Participating)

Year	Whites	Blacks
1972	35.7	19.1
1973	36.9	21.3
1974	37.6	22.4
1975	38.4	20.0
1976	37.2	17.7
1977	38.6	21.8
1978	40.9	25.5
1979	40.3	24.1
1980	42.0	22.4
1981	41.6	22.2
1982	36.7	21.0
1983	37.5	17.7
1984	39.6	17.3

*These people list going to school as their major activity.

Source: U.S. Department of Labor, *Employment and Earnings*, Table A-6, various issues.

with 1979 or 1984), so it is not clear from the data presented in the table whether the differential is narrowing or growing. The *levels* of participation have grown over the decade for both races. A simple eyeball analysis suggests that the racial *difference* has not been changing much, in either absolute or relative terms, falling from 46.5 percent of the white rate in 1972 to 39.5 percent in 1982 but rising to 56.3 percent of the white rate by 1984.

To summarize, it seems that black and white youth enroll in school in about the same proportions. Blacks in school are much less likely to be labor force participants than are whites, however, though the black rate is rising. Consequently, the evidence in tables 2.6 and 2.7 lends little support to the hypothesis that school enrollment rates explain the differential trends in labor force participation of 16- to 19-year-old males since 1972. Likewise, the fact that the participation rate of students is cyclically sensitive is not useful in explaining the differences in the volatility in participation. If the participation of black students is more cyclically sensitive than that of white students, that does not "explain" the racial difference in volatility. This may be an irrelevant distinction, since, as Gustman and Steinmeier (1981) show, the participation of white students is more cyclically sensitive than the participation of blacks. It is possible that the argument made by Bowen and Finegan (1969), that black youth who work while in school do so *in order to afford to go to school,* explains this. Given a desire to stay in school, they will be less likely to drop out of the labor force in response to a decrease in aggregate demand. There may be trouble in the interpretation of the Gustman and Steinmeier result, however. The result that they report is that the probability of being in the labor force, *given that they are in school,* is more cyclically responsive for whites than for blacks. If black youth's *school enrollment* is more responsive to cyclic conditions than that of white's, then the interpretation of the conditional probability reported is not clear. As aggregate demand rises, black youth labor market participation may in fact increase (just like that of white students), but they drop out of school to do it. Gustman and Steinmeier argue that such is the case. The results they report do not account for that effect, and the cross-section data set they use does not allow a direct test of the hypothesis, so the results must be interpreted with care. Edwards (1976) reports results that support the hypothesis that black enrollment rates are more cyclically sensitive than white rates, and that they do in fact vary procyclically (i.e., they rise as unemployment rates fall), so Gustman and Steinmeier may be correct. They argue that the effect arises from black students having a preference for full-time employment. This could arise because they on average have less wealth. Another reason is that as unemployment rates rise the probability that the sole breadwinner in the family becomes unemployed is greater for blacks than for whites, since black youth more than white youth are from single, female-headed households.[6] Whether the school-to-participation transitions are into full-time employment or not is therefore an important topic for further research. The evidence provided by Duncan (1965) suggests that the transitions are into part-time employment, at least for high school dropouts.

The Role of the Military

A story similar to the "school enrollment hypothesis" is based on the fact that black military enrollments have risen relative to whites over the past decade. The argument goes that "blacks are participating less because they are in the military more." Again, the question of why the military has become more attractive, and relatively moreso for blacks, has not been answered. Further research must address that issue. As a test of the relevance of the hypothesis, though, I have estimated the following regression equation

$$\log(\text{TOTLFPR})_t = \beta_0 + \beta_1 \text{TIME}_t + \Gamma(\text{seasonal dummies}) + u_t, \quad (2.1)$$

for 16- to 19-year-old males, for the January 1972 to December 1981 period. The variable TOTLFPR is the participation rate for the "total" noninstitutional population, defined to be the civilian population plus the military population. The "total labor force" is the civilian labor force plus the military population. TOTLFPR for age/race group i is therefore the total labor force for group i as a percent of the total group i population. The means and standard deviations of monthly data on TOTLFPR over the 1972–81 period are presented in table 2.8,

18   *The Participation Rate Differentials*

Table 2.8. Summary Statistics, "Total" Labor Force Participation Rate, 16–19-Year-Old Males

	Blacks	Whites
Mean (in percent)	46.81	64.31
Standard Deviation	8.76	7.39

for 16- to 19-year-old males. The measure indicates that blacks still participate less than whites. Further, the labor force participation rates, after adjustment for military enrollments, still exhibit the differential trends according to race. The results of estimating the trend coefficients from the equation above, using the "total" labor force participation rate data, are presented in table 2.9. They indicate that the trends do still exist. The total labor force participation rate has risen for white male youth, while it has fallen for black male youth. Black youth may be enlisting in the service at higher rates than before, but not enough to quell the divergent participation rate trends. As a result, the distinction between total and civilian participation may have little bearing on this research, and will hereafter be ignored.

Table 2.9. Regression Results: Equation (2.1) Dependent Variable: "Total" Labor Force Participation Rate, 16–19-Year-Old Males (in Logs)

	Blacks	Whites
CONSTANT	3.799*	4.097*
TIME	−.0007*	.0003*
R^2	.856	.950
D.W.	2.067	2.031

*Significant at the 95 percent level of confidence or greater.

Other Reasons

Again, neither increased school enrollment rates nor military enlistments is a "reason" for the decline in labor force participation among black youth. The military, and maybe to a lesser extent schooling, can be viewed as substitutes for the labor force, just as can helping out at home, or hustling on the street. The goal of research on that topic must be to identify reasons why the relative attractiveness of these alternatives has risen, or put differently, why the attractiveness of work has declined for blacks relative to whites. I argue that a primary reason is that civilian sector employment opportunities and hence expected wages are much lower and more volatile for blacks than for whites. Of course, there are many other factors that can be proposed in explanation of the participation rate differentials.

One possible explanation for the decline in black participation is that the utility that can be enjoyed while out of the labor force, the value of one's "nonmarket time," has risen for blacks over the decade. This can arise from changes in wealth or other sources of nonlabor income, family responsibilities, etc. The youth who has recently become a father is much more likely to be a member of the labor force than one who has no children, for instance. And there is seldom a million dollar lottery winner who does not take at least a few months off from work for that long-awaited vacation. As Iden (1980) points out, however, the proportion of young black males with family responsibilities has fallen over the past decade. Hence, black youth should be less likely to "need" employment, rather than more likely. In March of 1983, only .4 percent of black males aged 15 to 19 years had ever been married, compared to 2.1 percent of whites.[7] Differences in wealth would probably also lead black youth to participate more, rather than less, than white youth. Differences in other sources of nonlabor income, however, may be of more importance. For many poor families, nonlabor income can be a major source of wealth, whether in the form of cash from the Aid to Families with Dependent Children program, or food stamps. The proportion of AFDC recipients that is black is lower than the proportion that is white, however, and had fallen between 1975 and 1979 (see table 2.10), which would suggest that the labor force participation of blacks should have risen, not fallen over the period, in response to having relatively less nonlabor income. Of course table 2.10 does not indicate that the *incidence* of receipt of aid has fallen for blacks over the period, so that we should not totally discount its effects. Results presented by Plotnick (1983) suggest, however, that the propensity to enroll in AFDC programs is independent of race alone. In addition, the monthly per family AFDC payment fell during the 1972–80 period in real terms. In June of 1980, the average monthly payment to families was $288, up from $192 in 1972, an increase of 50 percent. But the Consumer Price Index rose by 94.6 percent over the same period. This

Table 2.10. Percent Distribution of AFDC Recipients

	1975	1977	1979
Percent White	50.2	52.6	51.7
Percent Black	44.3	43.0	43.9
Percent Others	5.5	4.4	4.4

Source: U.S. Bureau of the Census, *Statistical Abstract of the United States*, 1981.

should lead to an increase in labor supply, not a decrease. Of course, AFDC payments are not the only source of nonlabor income received by families of black youth. Other sources include food stamps, school lunch subsidies, rent subsidies, medicare, and medicaid. Racial differences in the incidence of participation in these programs are presented in table 2.11, for 1981. As with the AFDC program, blacks are more likely to receive aid than are whites.

Table 2.11. Incidence of Aid, by Race, 1981

Type of Aid	Percent of Households (H) or Population (P) Receiving Aid	
	Blacks	Whites
Food Stamps (H)	28.1	6.1
School Lunch (H)	50.4	14.9
SSI Total (P)*	3.8	1.2

*Includes AFDC.

Source: U.S. Department of Commerce, *Statistical Abstract of the United States*, 1986.

Another important source of nonlabor income for a worker in a household is the earnings of other household members. Racial differences in trends in the employment of the teenagers' parents, for instance, could contribute to the observed participation trends. The most obvious example is the increased labor supply of prime-aged women over the decade of the seventies. As more women work, it is less likely that male teenagers in the same households will work.[8] To the extent that black women have always worked, though, and since the increase in participation among women in the past decades has been primarily among white women, the increased participation of women does not seem a viable explanation for the decline in black youth labor market activity.[9] However, racial differences in the cyclic behavior of family members' employment may contribute to observed differences in participation volatility. If the primary wage earner in black households is more likely to suffer a decrease in earnings in a recession than his or her counterpart in white households, then black teens may respond differently in recessions than white teens. This logic would lead us to expect, though, that the black youth would increase their participation by more (or decrease it by less) than their white counterparts as aggregate demand fell. The results of our analysis presented in chapter 3 suggest that just the opposite occurs.

In addition to their earnings, simply whether or not other household members work can influence the labor supply of youth. If anything, having other household members working "sets a good example" for youth. Freeman (1983) reports that an important determinant of "who escapes" from poverty is the number of other members of the family who work. He does not find support, however, for the commonly held notion that the female-headed household is a "major deterrent to socioeconomic success." His results suggest that youths from homes in which both parents are present do only "marginally better," in terms of the amount of time they spend on "socially productive activities" (which includes work), than do those from homes in which only one parent is present. Indeed, "having some males in the household who are *not* employed appears to have negative effects."[10] In the context of the standard labor supply model, "setting a good example" serves either to decrease the value of leisure or increase the value of income from work, both of which lead to an increase in labor supply. In a sense the effect is equivalent to that produced by a greater "work ethic." Andrisani (1977) explores the issue of whether blacks and whites have different levels of the work ethic to some extent in his analysis of racial differences in internal-external attitudes. As defined by Rotter (1966), a worker possesses "internal attitudes" if he perceives effort to be instrumental in the attainment of success. He is "highly external" if, on the other hand, he ascribes little or no value to initiative, since success is viewed as being "completely unrelated to ability and effort."[11] Andrisani found that for men aged 16 to 26 years in 1968, blacks exhibited only a slight tendency to be less internal in their outlooks than whites. He concludes that "there is clearly little in these racial differences to support the contention . . . that the greater incidence of poverty among blacks might be explained in terms of a lower tendency to possess an internal outlook and Protestant work ethic."[12] In their study of the role of attitudes and aspirations in the determination of labor supply, Datcher-Loury and Loury (1983) find no relation between attitudes such as "working at a job is very important" or "the unemployed could find work if they wanted to" and hours or weeks worked for 16- to 19-year-old black males. They did not present any evidence of whether these attitudes differed according to race. Along the same lines, Freeman finds that "church going" is an important determinant of black teens' allocation of time between productive and unproductive activities. But unless we argue that blacks go to church less than whites and that this difference is growing, then there is little role for church-going as an explanation of the participation differentials. The evidence suggests that, if anything, blacks attend church more than whites. Of the National Longitudinal Survey respondents analyzed by Freeman, only 19 percent of the black youth reported they do not attend church at all, compared to 24 percent of the white youth. For blacks, 21 percent attend church once a week, compared to 20 percent for whites. Further, Datcher-Loury and Loury found that the attitude that "religion plays an important role in one's life" has no effect on black teenage labor supply. Of course the relationships between religious attitudes, church-going, internal-external attitudes, and the work ethic are not entirely clear. But each of these variables does reflect to some degree the extent to which the youth desire to be a part of the mainstream of society, as represented by the labor market. The evidence suggests that black and white youth are not very different in those desires. One final piece of evidence which supports this view is found in measures of the job market "aspirations" of youth. When asked "What type of job or occupation would you like to have when you are 30 years old?" black and white youth from the National Longitudinal Survey differ very little in their responses (see Datcher-Loury and Loury, 1983; or Holzer, 1986a).

Another source of the racial differences in participation could be linked to racial differences in levels and changes in the costs of search. If blacks utilize methods of search that are more costly than those used by whites, for instance, it is possible that they will participate less. Costs of search may be higher for blacks than for whites also because blacks tend to travel farther distances than whites for interviews as a result of their central city location. Recent evidence suggests that black and white youth show no significant differences in their job search methods, however (Bowers, 1979; Osterman, 1980; Holzer, 1986c), so that we can discount the first explanation. In table 2.12, I have presented data from Bowers' table 6. Though there are minor differences by race, the table suggests that in general blacks and whites exhibit the same search behavior; most

Table 2.12. Job Search Methods
(Method Used to Obtain Current Job)
16–19-Year-Olds, January 1973

	Percent Using Method	
Method Used	Whites	Blacks and Others
State Employment Agency	3.3	6.9
Private Employment Agency	1.7	—
Contact Employer Directly	34.5	26.4
Friends	30.1	21.8
Relatives	13.2	13.8
Answered Ads	5.5	6.9
Civil Service Test	.4	—
Teacher or Professor	1.3	2.3
School Placement Office	4.1	9.2
Other	5.9	12.7

Source: Bowers (1979), Table 6.

youth search for jobs by directly asking employers if they have jobs, and by asking friends and relatives (77.8 percent for whites, 62 percent for blacks). For all males 16 and over, the same patterns exist, as is shown in table 2.13. In addition, the data in the table suggests that there were not any significant trends in search behavior in the past decade that differ by race. There is not, therefore, any support for the hypothesis that blacks use more costly search methods than whites do, nor that they have exhibited a trend in that direction.

Table 2.13. Job Search Methods
Unemployed Males, 16 Years Old and Over, 1971–86

	Percent Using Method							
	Whites				Blacks and Others			
Method Used	1971	1975	1979	1986	1971	1975	1979	1986
Public Employment Agency	32.2	30.4	26.4	26.2	44.6	37.3	35.7	29.9
Private Agency	10.7	7.1	6.3	7.3	7.6	6.2	7.0	5.9
Direct Contact	73.3	72.5	73.3	74.7	66.8	69.8	68.7	74.4
Friends or Relatives	17.5	17.1	16.4	20.0	17.4	17.9	15.5	19.8
Placed or Answered Ads	25.6	29.2	29.2	35.8	18.4	21.9	23.1	30.5
Other	9.2	8.7	8.1	6.2	8.3	7.1	7.1	4.7
Average Number of Methods Used	1.68	1.65	1.60	1.70	1.63	1.60	1.57	1.65

Source: U.S. Department of Labor, *Employment and Earnings*, various issues.

This does not mean that we can ignore the costs of search argument, however, for a given method of search may be more expensive for blacks than for whites. For example, it may be more expensive for blacks to contact employers directly simply because they are farther away. Certainly central city employment opportunities have declined relative to those in the suburbs.[13] Alexis and DiTomaso (1983) find that blacks travel longer distances to get to work than whites, and that it takes significantly longer time. At the same time, though, the effect of this on participation is not clear, for they also find that black jobseekers are *willing* to spend significantly more time and to travel significantly farther distances to find jobs than are white jobseekers. Blacks pay higher costs, but also are willing to do so in order to find a job. The Alexis and DiTomaso results do not necessarily imply that costs of search have no effect on participation, though, for their sample was made up of individuals *who had decided to participate.* The results are not inconsistent, therefore, with the hypothesis that higher costs lead blacks to participate less than whites.

Black youth have been said to participate less than white youth and to have decreased their participation over the past decade also because they refuse to be a part of a market that offers them only low pay and menial work (for the best statement of this view, see E. Anderson, 1980). The idea is that they have increased their expectations (and hence demands) about wages and nonpecuniary aspects of jobs, due to increased educational levels, or, if you want, "black power." Though Morse (1980) seems to reject the hypothesis, his results are tentative and suggest that further research is necessary. Recent papers by Borus (1982) and Holzer (1986a) provide indirect evidence, however, in support of Morse. In a National Longitudinal Survey conducted in 1979, black and white youth were asked: Would you accept a full-time job doing [job] at a wage of [$2.50, $3.50, $5.00] per hour? The set of possible jobs was: washing dishes, working in a factory, working as a cleaning person, working at a check-out counter in a supermarket, working at a hamburger place, cleaning up neighborhoods, and working in a national forest or park, where the last two jobs were "public sector" in nature. Borus reports that "black youth showed significantly greater willingness to take all five of the private-sector jobs" at both $2.50 and at $5.00 per hour. For some reason, blacks were less willing than whites to clean up neighborhoods at $2.50 per hour, though the differential disappeared when they were offered $5.00. Holzer (1986b) reports that the "reservation wages" of unemployed black and white youth are comparable, on average, for the 1979–80 NLS sample ($4.22 and $4.30, respectively). Certainly the data does not indicate whether or not there has been any *trend* in their willingness to work, but it would be difficult to conclude from these results that blacks were less willing to work than whites in 1979.

From the standard labor supply analysis, probably the most important determinant of participation is the expected wage that workers can receive if employed. Recall that the "expected wage" has at least two dimensions. First is the actual wage payment received by employed workers, w. But unless we assume that all workers who want jobs are able to find jobs, then the wage that a given worker deciding to enter the labor force can "expect" to receive is the actual wage times the probability that he will find a job if he looks, p. The first component, the wage paid, does little to explain the divergence in black and white participation rates, at least in the 1970s. Most authors (especially Freeman (1981, 1978, 1975)) will agree that black and white wages are not significantly different, at entry, for the more recent age groups. One reason this is true for the age group studied here, of course, is that a large proportion of the jobs offered to teenagers pay the standard minimum wage. Because the proportions covered by the wage, by race, have not changed much in the past decade we see a good bit of convergence in earnings. In 1974, 87.4 percent of the workers covered by the minimum wage were white; 11.5 percent were black. In 1980, the rates were 87.9 and 11 percent, respectively.[14]

It can be argued, though, that the relevant wage variable for the labor supply decision is not only the wage that is offered in the current period, but rather that wage adjusted for the potential, future growth in wages that can be expected in the job, or some measure of lifetime wealth. As Lazear (1979) argues, much of the gains received by blacks in the form of increased entry-level wages has been at the expense of on-the-job-training and, thus, expected wage growth. One characteristic of the "menial job" cited in the discussion of the increased expectations hypothesis is that it offers no chance for advancement and growth.[15] Hence, blacks may participate less than whites because the expected wealth associated with employment is less than for whites. Trends in these wealth effects can have contributed to the trends in participation. But it is not clear that the current-wage/wage-growth distinction is a relevant one for young workers, anyway, who are notorious, regardless of race, for their low levels of "job-market attachment" and high turnover rates. As Gordon (1976) points out, most teenagers are not in search of permanent employment. Of course it is difficult to sort out cause and effect here, for teens' higher turnover rates may be the result of lower expected earnings.[16] Regardless, unless black and white teens differ in their desires for permanence in work, the wealth argument is probably not important. No evidence has been presented to suggest that this is so.

Wachter (1972, 1978) and Wachter and Kim (1982) have put forth a hypothesis regarding the relationship between wages and labor force participation that is quite different. They argue that workers in the secondary sector of the labor market, primarily women and teenagers, suffered relative earnings losses over the decades of the sixties and seventies (as compared to workers in the primary sector). Because they desire to maintain a constant level of relative consumption, they are forced to work more as a result. Essentially an income effect, the notion works well to explain the increased participation of women over the past decade, as the results presented in Wachter (1978) suggest. It contributes little, however, to our understanding of the behavior of youth over the same period, particularly the *decline* in participation of blacks.

Of course, not all rewards from work are in the form of wage payments, whether current, future, or relative to the payments of others. In addition to wages, workers receive payments in the form of fringe benefits, and are compensated for low incomes through safer, cleaner, and more satisfying work.[17] The total of the wage and nonpecuniary rewards from work may sufficiently be distributed toward whites such that work is relatively less attractive for blacks. Trends in nonpecuniary differences could help to explain the differential trends in participation. The evidence that such differences exist is mixed. Duncan (1976) finds from the 1972–73 Quality of Employment Survey that blacks rank lower than whites in terms of the amount of "job autonomy" and "control over overtime hours" associated with their jobs. They rank higher, though, in terms of other job characteristics, including "fringe benefits" and "health and safety." Kaun (1975), using data from the 1960 U.S. Census, found that after controlling for years of education and the intelligence, verbal, and numerical requirements demanded by the job, blacks have "less challenging" work than do whites. The disparities decrease with years of education, however. Because educational levels of blacks have risen relative to whites in the past twenty years, these disparities may have decreased. Neither of the two studies controlled for differences in wages of the workers. It is not clear to what extent differences in individual characteristics of jobs are important, however. The notion of "total job satisfaction" may be a more important variable. Bartel (1981) finds from NLS data for mature men that in response to the question "How do you feel about your job?" (like it much, like it fairly well, etc.), blacks were significantly more "satisfied" with their jobs in 1971 than were whites. She reports that in 1966 the reverse was true. Clearly we cannot conclude from this that the black youth of 1980 were more satisfied with their jobs than were their white comrades. The "increased expectations" hypothesis would suggest just the opposite to be true. And, as Bartel argues, blacks may simply have come over time to be satisfied by lower returns than whites. She attempts to break the response into parts due to the preferences of the workers and those due to differences in the levels of rewards received, and finds support for that hypothesis. If blacks and whites did not "evaluate" their rewards differently, her results suggest that blacks would indeed report lower levels of job satisfaction than whites. Again, though, we have no evidence of trends in these effects.

Each of the many items discussed above may have contributed to the observed divergence in black and white participation rates. But to me the most important reason cited for black-white differences in participation stems from racial differences in the "nonreturn" component of the expected wage: the expected probability of finding a job, p, or employment opportunities in general.[18] We can form many hypotheses using this variable. Blacks' participation rates may be lower than whites' because employment opportunities are lower for blacks than for whites. The participation rates may have declined for black teenagers because of a secular decline in their employment prospects. It is straightforward to conclude also that the greater volatility in participation exhibited by blacks is the result of greater volatility in employment opportunities.

Evidence in support of the first two hypotheses is presented in figure 2.2, where I've plotted the monthly, seasonally adjusted unemployment rates for the two groups for the 1972–85 period. The data suggests that black male teenage unemployment rates are higher than those of white youth, and that the black rate has risen over the sample period. The results of a regression of the unemployment rate on TIME are presented in table 2.14. They suggest a significant, secular

Figure 2.2. Black and White Male Teenage Unemployment Rates, 1972–85

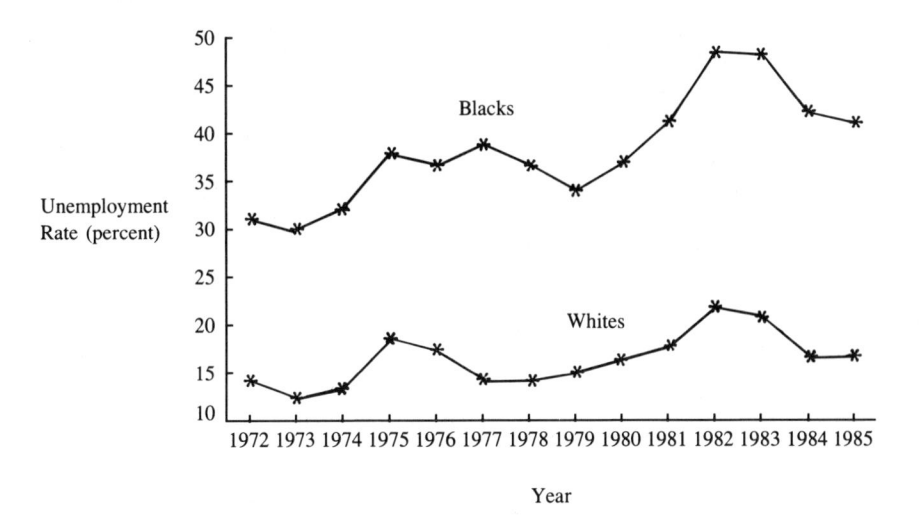

Table 2.14. Time Trend Estimates
Dependent Variable = Monthly Unemployment
Rate, 1972–85

Independent Variable	Coefficient (t-Statistic) Blacks	Coefficient (t-Statistic) Whites
CONSTANT	29.5526*** (12.454)	10.1826*** (2.673)
TIME	0.1369** (2.173)	0.1175 (1.338)
TIME2	−0.0003 (−0.806)	−0.0005 (−1.032)
R^2	.171	.020
F	16.921	1.699
D.W.	2.409	2.381

*** Significant at a 99 percent level of confidence or greater.
 ** Significant at a 95 percent level of confidence or greater.
  * Significant at a 90 percent level of confidence or greater.

28 The Participation Rate Differentials

decline in the employment opportunities faced by blacks, as evidenced by the secular increase in the unemployment rate. Summary statistics for the deviations from trend are presented in table 2.15. Referring to the table, black teenagers' unemployment rates do seem very volatile, and more so than that of their white counterparts (standard deviations for the raw data of 6.23 and 2.81 respectively).

Table 2.15. Descriptive Statistics: Deviations from Trend in Black and White Male Teenage Unemployment Rates, 1972–85

	Standard Deviation	
	Blacks	Whites
Raw Data	6.225	2.811
Pre-YEDPA	4.623	2.378
Post-YEDPA	5.716	2.864
Detrended Data	3.503	0.903
Pre-YEDPA	3.774	0.766
Post-YEDPA	3.331	0.981
Percent Deviation from Trend Data	9.312	5.618
Pre-YEDPA	11.271	5.105
Post-YEDPA	7.858	5.930

Note: These estimates are for monthly, seasonally adjusted unemployment rates. The "detrended data" were computed using the specifications in table 2.14.

Summary and Concluding Remarks

Economic theory predicts that racial differences in levels and rates of change in labor force participation rates are due to (1) racial differences in levels or rates of change in costs of search, nonlabor income, the wage received when employed, and the probability of employment, and (2) differences in worker preferences for income and leisure. Evidence that black youth face higher costs, receive lower rates of pay, or have less desire or need for work than white youth is scarce or mixed. The fact that they face a lower probability of being employed given that they do participate, as measured by their unemployment rate, cannot be denied. It is therefore clear that, in order to understand the participation rate differentials (in levels, trends, and volatility), we must identify the reasons that racial differences in levels, trends, and variations in employment opportunities exist.

Sources of Differences in Employment Opportunities

In a simple labor market model, the level of employment or unemployment (or the probability that a worker is employed or unemployed) at a point in time is determined by the interaction of the demand for workers (determined by the firms' perceptions of worker productivities and the demand for the firms' output) and the number of workers willing to accept employment at the wages offered to them by firms (the supply). If either of these factors differs according to race, then we would expect employment to differ according to race. One other source of employment inequality stems from the fact that blacks and whites may not be distributed equally across industries or sectors of the economy. We will discuss the roles of each of these three factors in explaining the unequal distribution of employment and unemployment among black and white teenagers in turn.

Differences in Supply

One of the determinants of the number of teenage workers willing to work at a given wage rate (the supply of workers) is simply the total number of teenagers. Trends in the growth of the teenage populations could therefore contribute to their increasing employment problems, and to the racial differences I have noted. Bowers (1979) notes that between 1964 and 1976 the black teenage population grew at a rate of 4.3 percent per year, compared with a rate of 2.3 percent for whites.[19] Although the relative rate of population growth for teenagers as a whole has declined since mid-1977,[20] the black rate has continued to grow into the 1980s. The notion that the "baby-boom" has served to decrease employment prospects for teenagers as a group in the 1960s and 1970s is generally accepted. Dernberg and Strand (1966) and Iden (1976, 1980) find that the relative population share of young workers significantly depresses their employment (or increases their unemployment) rates. According to Iden (1976), "the increase in the relative size of the teenage group may have added as much as 3.9 percentage points" to their unemployment rate between 1954 and 1975. Both Iden (1980) and Ragan (1977) have found that the importance of the relative population share variable is greater for blacks than for whites. Indeed, for males, Ragan consistently finds that the growth in their population has no effect at all on the employment probability for whites, while for blacks it has significant, negative effects. Iden's results, on the other hand, indicate that the differential effect by race is primarily among women.

Interpreting these results is not easy. The relationship between population share and employment share depends on the substitutability of teens for other groups in the labor market, and on whether the market is free to adjust to the increased supply. As Ragan notes, "If wages are sufficiently flexible, an increase in relative youth population need not increase unemployment rates."[21] Mincer (1966) writes that "the population explosion has been blamed for sins it does not perpetrate without accomplices," referring to low teenage productivity and the minimum wage.[22] The racial differences in the effect of the supply of teens therefore indicate either that firms perceive the productivity of black workers to be lower than that of white workers, or that blacks' wages are less flexible than whites'. The first factor will be discussed in the context of differences in the demands for workers. The fact that teens' wages are rigid downward, and arguably so because of the minimum wage, seems apparent. There is no evidence that the degree of stickiness varies according to race, however. In sum, the argument that black employment prospects have fallen relative to those of whites as a result of the baby boom is telling only half the story.

Of course the other determinant of the "total supply of workers" lies not in the number of workers, but rather in their willingness to work at various wages. This willingness differs from the "willingness to participate" already discussed, in that here we assume that the workers have already made the decision to be in the labor force. The issue now is whether they are employed or unemployed. Racial differences (and trends) in the propensity for employment could obviously be linked to racial differences in the propensity to accept wage offers when unemployed. The "increased expectations" hypothesis has direct bearing on this point. Standard models of "job search" behavior imply that nonlabor income (e.g., AFDC payments, or most notably, unemployment insurance payments) should also have effects on the propensity to leave unemployment. I argued above that the results presented by Morse (1981), Borus (1982), and Holzer (1986a) lend little support to the notion that blacks are "less willing" to work than whites are, however, and that they especially do not seem to demand higher wages than whites. Holzer (1986b) finds, however, that black youth do tend to demand higher wages than they can expect to earn, but this reflects differential demand more than supply. Because much teenage unemployment occurs upon initial entry into the labor force, unemployment insurance probably is not an important deterrent to teenage employment, either. Clearly we should not expect racial differences in its effect. And hypotheses regarding the effects of wealth and other forms of nonlabor income would lead us to expect that whites, not blacks, would tend to search longer and exhibit higher unemployment rates. In short, none of these "supply-side" factors seems to contribute much to our understanding of the racial differential in employment.

A related and probably more important factor is the notion that black workers are *less efficient searchers* than are whites. Weiner (1982) and Flanagan (1978) offer this as an explanation for racial differences in adult male unemployment. Recall from the discussion of "costs of search," that evidence suggests that blacks and whites employ essentially the same search methods. Still, this does not mean that they yield the same results. Osterman (1980) points out that friends and relatives are a primary source of job information, regardless of race. Osterman notes also, though, that "contacts for whites may simply be more effective" than those for blacks. "Assuming that the peers and family of youth are similar to themselves, a smaller fraction of these contacts for blacks will be employed than for whites and thus the network may be less efficacious."[23] Holzer (1986c) has found that the "effectiveness" of job search methods is significantly less for blacks. From a different perspective, however, Dayton (1981) finds that though blacks and whites again use the same search methods, "Whites appear to more often analyze their interests and abilities to select the right job for themselves and to select a specific job to look for" than do blacks.[24] This could be an important contributor to the black employment problem. It is not clear, though, how it contributes to the trends.

To summarize, it seems that the labor supply-side offers little in explanation of the black-white employment and unemployment rate differentials and their growth, except to the extent that blacks are less efficient searchers than are whites. There is little support for the hypotheses that black youth are less willing to work than their white counterparts at the wages being offered because of increased expectations, nor that they have higher reservation wages because they have more wealth or other nonlabor income. Indeed, blacks have slightly lower reservation wages.

Differences in the Demand for Workers

The quantity of workers demanded by a firm at a given wage is an increasing function of the productivity of the workers. Productivity is not always easily measured, however, so that factors that affect employers' *perceptions* of workers' productivity come to be important determinants of the number of workers hired.[25] This is particularly important for workers that have little or no previous employment experience, like teenagers. An employer must then make predictions about a worker's productivity on the job based on the worker's productivity in school, the school he went to, where he lives, his personality, appearance, and race. The relationship between the worker's attributes and the employer's previous experience with similar workers determines the worker's expected productivity and hence whether he is offered a job. In addition, some employers may simply prefer to employ workers of a particular sex or race. This last factor, labor market discrimination resulting from prejudice, may be an important contributor to the black teenage employment problem and will underly much of the following discussion.[26] We begin, though, with a discussion of the most generally accepted determinants of productivity: schooling, experience, native ability, and, again, the work ethic. Our goal, again, is to explain the fact that blacks have a much lower probability of employment than do whites; the special goal here is to ask if it is because blacks are less productive.

If so, it certainly is not because they have less education, at least for the younger age group. As we saw in table 2.6, black and white teenagers enroll in school at about the same rates. Furthermore, total educational attainment levels seem to have converged. The median "years of school completed" for 20- to 24-year-old blacks in 1979 was 12.5 years. The median for whites was 12.8. The percent of black 20- to 24-year-olds that had completed four years of high school (but not gone on to college) was 45 percent in 1979, compared to 43.3 percent for their white peers.[27] Recall that increased relative educational levels were cited as a source of black youth's "rising expectations" regarding wages. In all, it is fairly safe to conclude that any black and white productivity differences which may exist do not arise from differences in schooling levels.

Of course, it is possible that the *quality* of the schooling received by blacks is lower than that received by whites, and that the differential has grown over the past decade. Welch (1973) argues that racial trends have been *toward* educational equality rather than away from it, however, and the recent math, reading, and science achievement scores (presented in tables 2.17−2.19) suggest that those trends have continued through the 1970s and perhaps into the 1980s. Still, these measures are not perfect, and may not at all measure quality as perceived by employers. But even if the quality of schooling should be measured according to its effectiveness in preparing youth to be disciplined, obedient, and punctual, there is little evidence to suggest that it has declined for blacks relative to whites, particularly over the past decade.

It is true, however, that conventional measures of school quality indicate that schooling for blacks has been deficient. Black youth have historically had a higher propensity for illiteracy, for instance, than have whites, though the differential has narrowed considerably, as is indicated in table 2.16. In addition, blacks consistently score worse than whites in reading, mathematics, and science tests. This is shown in table 2.17, for the National Assessment of Educational Progress tests. But this differential also seems to be narrowing, at least for the reading and mathematics scores. Table 2.17 indicates that the black student in high school in the mid-1970s scored better (relative to whites) in all three subjects than did the cohort schooled in the early 1960s. One source of this tendency toward equality in performance could be the tendency toward equality in educational attainment

Table 2.16. Illiteracy Rates
Civilian, Noninstitutionalized Males, 14–24 Years Old

Percent of Population Illiterate		
Year	Blacks	Whites
1959	1.7	0.7
1969	0.6	0.3
1979*	0.2*	0.2*

*The figures for this year are for both men and women, and so are not directly comparable to the 1959 and 1969 figures.

Source: U.S. Bureau of the Census, *Statistical Abstract of the United States*, 1982–83.

Table 2.17. Deviations from National Average on NEAP Tests 17-Year-Olds, by Subject and Race, Various Years

	Reading		
	1970–71	*1974–75*	*1979–80*
Blacks	−16.9	−16.6	−16.6
Whites	2.3	2.8	2.9

	Science	
	1972–73	*1976–77*
Blacks	−12.6	−13.5
Whites	2.2	2.2

	Mathematics		
	1972–73	*1977–78*	*1981–82*
Blacks	−18.2	−17.2	−15.2
Whites	2.8	2.9	2.9

Source: *Digest of Educational Statistics*, 1986.

of the youth's parents. Students whose parents had graduated from high school perform significantly better than those whose parents had not. This is shown in table 2.18. The blame for poor performance by blacks therefore should not be placed on the schools exclusively. The results reported by Jencks (1972) suggest that differences in the quality of schooling contribute very little in explanation for differences in earnings, anyway. Of course, it could be argued that blacks perform worse in school and in the labor market simply because they have less native ability. The fact that blacks have historically scored worse on intelligence tests than whites is consistent with that view. And high IQ people reap greater rewards in the job market (in income, at least) than those with low IQs.[28] But racial biases in and more general problems in the interpretation of test scores as measures of ability as opposed to measures of achievement are well known.[29] Further, racial differences in reading, math, and science scores seem to grow with age, as is evidenced in table 2.19, which suggests that the differences we observe at age 17 are not attributable only to ability, and point again to deficiencies in schooling. Furthermore, the differentials, for all ages, seem to have declined over time.

In sum, the hypotheses that the quality of education is lower for blacks than for whites and that blacks perform less well in school and show lower levels of achievement in reading, science, and math than do whites do find some support. The differentials have narrowed rather than grown over the past decade, however,

34 *The Participation Rate Differentials*

Table 2.18. Deviations from National Average on NEAP Tests 17-Year-Olds, by Parental Education and Subject, 1975–82

Parental Education	Reading	Science	Mathematics
Not High School Graduate	−8.6	−8.0	−9.9
High School Graduate	−2.2	−1.8	−2.0
Post High School	3.4	5.1	2.9

Source: *Digest of Educational Statistics*, various issues.

Table 2.19. Deviations from National Average on NEAP Tests by Subject, Age, and Race, 1975–82

	Reading		
	Age 9 *(in 1970–71)*	*Age 13* *(in 1974–75)*	*Age 17* *(in 1979–80)*
Blacks	−14.3	−14.3	−16.6
Whites	2.4	2.8	2.9
	Mathematics		
	Age 9 *(in 1971–72)*	*Age 13* *(in 1977–78)*	*Age 17* *(in 1981–82)*
Blacks	−14.7	−18.2	−15.2
Whites	3.0	3.7	2.9

Source: *Digest of Educational Statistics*, various years.

such that they do not contribute to the growing employment differential of the past decade.

If a goal of schools is to instill in the students a work ethic, then the results presented by Andrisani could (except for my qualifications) indicate that schools have been successful, for both races. And it is clear that internal attitudes are rewarded in the labor market. Becker and Hills (1980, 1981) consistently find that teenagers with internal attitudes have both higher future earnings and shorter periods of unemployment than youth with external attitudes. It should be noted, however, that the slight racial differences in attitudes reported by Andrisani were found by Becker and Hills to contribute significantly to racial differences in unemployment experiences. It is not clear, however, whether that result is the product of the differences in attitudes alone, or also of employers' reactions to differences in attitudes. If it is the latter, and the attitudes are not productivity related, then the black unemployment problem could in part be due to racial discrimination.[30]

Another important contributor to the productivity of a worker is his or her previous labor market experience. In the jobs filled by teenagers, a significant part of the learning required occurs on the job, not in school. Though much of that training may be firm-specific in nature, at least some is general and is valued highly by employers. Because blacks are less likely to participate in the labor market, particularly black students, and because they have a higher unemployment probability and longer durations of unemployment given that they do participate, blacks will on average have less previous work experience than whites. To the extent that wages are fixed, this will result in lower levels of employment. The interaction of the two participation and unemployment rate trends then also works to ensure that we observe a downward trend in work experience for black youth. This is evident from the data presented in table 2.20. Two measures of experience are presented there. In column 1 is the percent of the male population 16 to 24 years old who have some work experience during the year. In column 2 is the percent of the 15- to 19-year-old male population with some earned

Table 2.20. Percent of Male Teenagers with Work Experience or Income during the Year, 1970–84

Year	White (1)	White (2)	Black and Other (1)	Black and Other (2)
1970	72.7	74.7	59.3	61.0
1971	70.5	*	54.7	*
1972	72.1	*	50.2	*
1973	75.1	*	57.6	*
1974	75.0	*	56.0	*
1975	70.1	73.2	47.2	52.7
1976	72.4	76.8	46.1	49.7
1977	73.8	78.1	47.2	51.9
1978	*	81.4	*	59.3
1979	*	78.0	*	52.6
1980	*	73.7	*	53.7
1981	*	74.7	*	47.6
1982	*	70.9	*	41.3
1983	*	71.5	*	44.4
1984	*	71.2	*	47.5

*Not available.

Column (1): percent of males 16 to 24 years old with work experience during the year. Source: Bowers (1979).

Column (2): percent of males 16 to 19 years old (except years 1979–84, which include 15-year-olds) with earned income during the year. Source: U.S. Census Bureau, *Current Population Reports*, Series P-60.

income during the year. Both measures suggest that black youth have experienced a significant decline in work experience over the past decade, especially when considered relative to whites. Of course once again cause and effect are difficult to identify. Regardless, a black teenager filling out job applications will probably have less work experience than an otherwise comparable white, and will be less desirable to employers as a result. In addition, the 'type''of experience that blacks receive may be different from that received by whites, and may not look as good on a resume. The argument made by Lazear, that black workers receive less on-the-job-training as a result of affirmative action programs, may manifest itself in the teenage market in the form of white youth receiving more demanding, "tenure track" employment. There is no evidence in support of this hypothesis, however, except that it could explain the result presented by Jud and Walker that, at least for blue-collar occupations, blacks receive much lower monetary returns-to-experience than do whites. Of course, that result could also be explained by some more overt form of discrimination.

Indeed, labor market discrimination can be argued to contribute to the racial difference in employment in a number of other ways. Any observed difference in the effect of a variable on employment, whether experience level or level of initiative, can be attributed at least in part to racial discrimination. Such differences have been found for teenagers in the effects of a number of variables: the minimum wage,[31] the postwar decline in military demands (Mincer, 1976; Betsey and Dunson, 1981; Iden, 1980), population growth rates (Ragan, 1977; Iden, 1980), and the business cycle (Clark and Summers, 1981). To the extent that other factors which determine the employment or unemployment rates of the demographic groups have been accounted for, the differential effects of the variables signify that black and white youth are "treated differently" in the labor market. In fact, some of the variables listed above (i.e., the relative minimum wage, or population share) should not be expected to have effects on the employment of teens over the past decade anyway, much less differential effects by race.[32] If the productivity of black and white youth is the same, then differential effects of labor market competition from women or immigrants (also seen to be a deterrent to youth employment in general) also would indicate discrimination.

Another way discrimination affects employment is through the "crowding" of blacks into occupations, industries, or sectors of the economy that offer both low wages and few, unstable, or declining employment opportunities.[33] For example, rural southern black youth have historically been attached to employment in agriculture. Cogan (1982) attributes a substantial part of the decline in black youth employment in the 1950s and 1960s to the decline in the agricultural demand for labor over the period resulting from technological innovations. But as O'Neill (1983) and Cogan both point out, the decline in black employment that has continued into the 1980s is not regional in nature and is not attributable to declining agricultural demands. Osterman (1980) reports that there also is little support for the "unstable employment" hypothesis. In his sample of teens in 1969–70, blacks averaged 3.39 weeks of unemployment. He calculates that they would have averaged 3.32 weeks of unemployment if they had had the same industrial distribution as whites, a reduction of only 2 percent.

A related and frequently heard explanation for black and white employment differences is the fact that blacks are heavily represented in central cities, while employment opportunities have increasingly become heavily represented in the suburbs. Because of lack of transportation to the suburbs or because of its high costs (and because of housing discrimination), these jobs are seen as unavailable for blacks. We saw above, though, that blacks do seem to be willing to make the lengthy trips that may be necessary to get those jobs. In addition, the work of Ellwood (1983), Cohen (1979), Westcott (1976), and Friedlander (1972) suggests that even suburban blacks are at a relative employment disadvantage when compared to whites. As Bowers notes, "The [employment] situation of blacks relative to whites does not seem to be specific to the central city."[34]

To summarize, the quality of schooling may be sufficiently lower for blacks such that they are less productive in the labor market. Blacks' performance in school has risen relative to whites' in recent years, however, so that the schooling hypothesis does not explain the divergent employment trends. Racial differences in work attitudes and previous work experience may contribute much to the employment differential, but their contributions to the trends also is not clear. It is clear that worker attitudes and experience depend to a large extent on the employment differential itself and so are endogenously determined, which creates problems for "causal" interpretations. An alternative explanation for the employment differential is that even though black and white youth are in fact equally productive, they are not treated as such in the labor market. Whether this arises from prejudice or simple employer ignorance about worker productivities is not important; both can lead to discrimination on the basis of race and put black youth at a significant disadvantage in the labor market.

One last explanation for racial differences in employment experiences is a "statistical" one. Mare and Winship (1983) argue that schools and the military draw the 'higher quality'' workers from the labor force. Because blacks have increased their tendency to participate in the military and school over the past few decades, lower quality workers are more heavily represented in the black labor force. The average quality of the black labor force therefore declines. We cannot conclude from their results that there is any support for the hypothesis, however, or that it is an important determinant of the black employment decline. Also, it is not clear that the hypothesis should be true in the context of a competitive model. The returns in the labor force should adjust in order to stop the flow into the military. In addition, the hypothesis is not really relevant for 16- to 19-year-olds, since most of them are not in the military. For the youngest workers the important question still is, "Why do black students have higher unemployment rates (less employment opportunity) than whites?" Even more important, though, as tables 2.6 and 2.7 indicated, the trend toward more school enrollment for blacks leveled off in the 1970s and black students have tended to participate in the labor market more, so that the hypothesis that the best black workers have been syphoned off by the schools seems least relevant for the teenagers of the past decade.

Concluding Remarks

There is much of the recent black-white employment differential that is not explained by the standard model of employment determination. Neither the supply nor the productivity characteristics of black workers explain much of their position relative to whites, nor its decline in the past decade. If any one conclusion stands out it is that employment discrimination is a major contributor to the black teenage employment problem. The goal of this book is not to explain teenage employment, however, but rather teenage participation. The survey above was intended only to outline the many factors that could, through their effects on employment opportunities, have contributed to the growth in the participation differential.

One such factor was the greater responsiveness for black teens of employment opportunities over the business cycle noted by Clark and Summers. I have argued that the greater volatility in black employment rates could be a major source of the greater volatility in black labor market participation. If that also leads to less accumulation of human capital through decreased work experience, then clearly it also contributes to the employment decline in general. A greater *responsiveness* in participation to given changes in employment prospects among blacks makes matters even worse. Recall that racial differences in $\delta r/\delta Z$ can result from racial differences in $\delta R/\delta Z$ or $\delta Z/\delta t$. I will show that a racial difference in the responsiveness of participation rates to changes in employment opportunities does in fact exist. This "differential discouraged worker effect" can be a major contributor to the black teenage employment problem in general.

Summary and Concluding Remarks

Black male teenagers participate in the labor market less than whites and the differences between them have been growing. The fact that employment opportunities for blacks decline more in business cycle downturns than do those for whites (as evidenced by the greater volatility of the black unemployment rate) and the fact that these declines elicit a proportionately greater decline in participation among blacks than among whites contribute to the fact that the participation rate is also more volatile for blacks than it is for whites. They may also contribute to the downward participation trend. Our evaluation of various hypotheses to explain these phenomena lead to the conclusion that military enrollments, school enrollments, income transfer payments, earnings differences, expectations about earnings and job satisfaction, and work attitudes all play little or no role in explaining black/white participation rate differences among male teenagers. Even the costs of search argument may be unimportant. The major source of the racial differentials in participation behavior seems to be the racial differentials in employment. The analysis further suggests that these teenage employment differentials may be attributed to racial differences in the quality of schooling (as measured by test score performance), work experience, and the effectiveness of search methods. A substantial portion should probably also be attributed to labor market discrimination against blacks.

As a result of these conclusions, we will concentrate on the relationships between "employment opportunities" and labor force participation rates.

3

Racial Differences in the Discouraged Worker Effect

This chapter presents evidence that the discouraged worker phenomenon contributed significantly to variations in the labor force participation rates of male teenagers during the past decade, and that the discouragement effect is stronger for blacks than for whites. To ascertain the "nature" of this differential effect, I also examine the cyclic behavior of the labor market flows which generate it.

Time Series Evidence of Differential Discouragement

The discouraged worker effect is defined throughout this study to be the observed decline in the labor force participation rate associated with a rise in the unemployment rate, or any other measure of aggregate economic activity used to proxy for employment opportunities in general. (Throughout this work I will use the unemployment rate.) In this first section I examine that relationship for black and white male teenagers, using the published unemployment and labor force participation rate data presented in chapter 2.

Previous Work

Empirical analysis of the relationship between cyclical changes in employment and cyclical changes in participation rates dates back at least to the work of Clarence Long in 1958. The decade which followed saw many extensions of that work, some nearly "classic," including the work of Tella (1964, 1965), Dernberg and Strand (1966), Bowen and Finegan (1965, 1969), and Jacob Mincer (1966). More recent analyses include those by Kaitz (1970), Perry (1977), and Clark and Summers (1981). Because they are the most directly related to the analysis in this section, I will discuss only the Tella, Dernberg and Strand, and Clark and Summers papers here.

The work by Tella (1965) and Dernberg and Strand first indicated that male teenagers exhibit strong, if not the strongest, participation responses to changes in employment rates. This result was subsequently confirmed by Mincer (1966), Bowen and Finegan (1969), Kaitz (1970), and Perry (1977). Using quarterly data covering the 1947:IV–1964:II period, Tella estimated, by age and sex, the regression coefficients in the following equation:

$$\left(\frac{L+A}{P}\right)_t^i = a + b_1 \left(\frac{E+A}{P}\right)_{t-1}^i + b_2 (\log T)_t, \qquad (3.1)$$

where L = the age-sex group i labor force, A = the group i armed forces enrollment, E = group i civilian employment, P = group i population, and T = time (1947:IV=100).

The cyclical coefficient, b_1, is taken to be a measure of the discouraged worker effect. Its value was estimated to be .358 for 14- to 19-year-old males. That is, a 1 percentage point increase in the male teenagers' employment to population ratio (e.g., from .60 to .61) is associated with an increase in their labor force participation rate of .358 percentage points (from .500 to .504). The coefficient was 9 times its own standard error, and more than 5 times the coefficient for 35–44 year olds.

Dernberg and Strand estimated, for each age-sex group i, the coefficients in the equation

$$\left(\frac{L_i}{P}\right)_t = a_{mi} + a_{1i}\left(\frac{E}{P}\right)_t + a_{2i}\left(\frac{X}{P}\right)_{t+2} + a_{3i}\left(\frac{1}{P}\right)_t + a_{4i}\left(\frac{P_i}{P}\right)_t + r_t, \qquad (3.2)$$

using monthly data for the 1952–62 period, where

    a_{mi} = a month specific intercept term,
    L_i = group i labor force,
    E = total employment,
    P = total population,
    P_i = group i population,
    and X = the total number of new unemployment compensation exhaustions.

Their results also confirm the discouraged worker hypothesis, and once again the teenage male coefficient was significantly larger than the coefficients for the other age and sex subgroups.

We should note that Tella's and Dernberg and Strand's specifications differ in a number of ways. First, Tella uses the age/sex group-specific employment ratio as his measure of aggregate demand, lagged one period, while Dernberg and Strand use the contemporaneous, aggregate rate. Both measures are used as solutions to the sampling error bias that would arise if contemporaneous group-specific rates were used. As Tella describes the problem, "it is very likely that the presence of the same sampling error in both employment and labor force in the coincident relationship" will introduce a spurious correlation between the two which biases the R^2's and the regression coefficient on the employment/population ratio variable. We should not, therefore, use time contemporaneous labor force and unemployment or employment rate data in the same regressions. A second difference between the two specifications is that Tella uses the group-specific labor force participation rate as the dependent variable, while Dernberg and Strand use what they call the "group labor force participation ratio," which measures the group-specific labor force relative to the *total* population. But even given these differences, both specifications support the hypothesis that the discouraged worker effect is a significant contributor to cyclical variations in male teenage labor force participation.

Clark and Summers (1981), in their study of the responsiveness of *employment* rates to cyclical conditions, also produced evidence that teenage participation rates are very responsive to changes in employment opportunities, and presented results by race. Using quarterly data for the 1950–76 period and regressions of the logs of participation rates on current and seven-period lags of the 35- to 44-year-old male unemployment rate, their results indicate that a 1 percentage point decrease in the mature male unemployment rate causes 2.03 and 2.38 percent increases in the black and white participation rates, respectively. Again, both coefficients are significantly different from zero at conventional levels of significance.

Previous work has shown, then, that changes in the levels of the unemployment and employment rates have significant influences on the participation rate for teenage males, though the response does not seem to differ much by race. Note, though, that Clark and Summers present *absolute* measures of the response of participation to changes in demand. Their results suggest that the *relative* response is much greater for blacks than for whites, since the black participation rate is much lower than the white rate. Certainly a relative measure, closer to an elasticity, is a better measure of the "strength" of the discouraged worker effect than is an absolute one. I will present both measures in the following analysis.

Extensions

We saw that labor force participation has been expressed as a function of some measure of "labor market tightness" or "employment opportunities," Z, and some vector of other exogenous variables, X, or $(L/P) = L(X,Z)$. I use a variant of this basic construct here. In particular, I estimate the coefficients for the equation

$$\left(\frac{L}{P}\right) = \beta_0 + \beta_1 \left(\frac{L}{P}\right)^i_{t-1} + \beta_2 \left(\frac{U}{L}\right)^i_{t-1} + \beta_3 \text{TIME} + \beta_4 \text{TIME2} + v_t, \quad (3.3)$$

where U is the level of unemployment and the "i" superscript indexes racial group. This formulation differs from previous work in a few ways. First is the exclusion of other exogenous variables. Examples of what has been included in other work are variables to take account of changes in transfer payments (e.g., the unemployment compensation variable used by Tella) and changes in the levels or rates of growth in population. I concentrate only on the unemployment rate in this chapter. The effects which other variables have on participation are examined in detail in chapters 5 and 6. Using the lagged value of the labor force participation rate as an explanatory variable is another deviation, suggested by Wachter (1977).

More important, I use the race-specific, own-age unemployment rate as the explanatory variable of concern. Dernberg and Strand, Kaitz, and Clark and Summers all used the prime-aged male or some aggregate rate as their measure of labor market tightness, in large part because of the sampling error bias noted above. I will avoid the sampling error problem by using the lagged, group-specific unemployment rate as the employment opportunities variable, as Tella had used the group-specific employment to population ratio. The group-specific rate is a much better proxy for group-specific perceptions of employment opportunities, and thus seems to be the most appropriate explanatory variable.

The estimated coefficients are presented in table 3.1, by race. The data used is the raw unemployment and participation rate data presented in chapter 2, for the 1972:01 to 1985:12 period. The significant negative coefficients for the unemployment rate variable support the discouraged worker hypothesis, for both races. The effect is strongest for whites, in accordance with the Clark and Summers results. That is, an increase in the unemployment rate by 1 percent (e.g., from 10 to 11 percent) would cause a decrease in the participation rate of 28.32 percentage points for whites (from 60 to 32.68), compared to a decrease of only 14.74 percentage points (from 40 to 25.26) for blacks.

As argued, a more appropriate measure of the "strength" of the discouraged worker effect is a relative one. Because blacks' unemployment rates are higher and participation rates are lower than those of whites, it is likely that the results presented in table 3.1 in fact signify a stronger relative response for blacks than for whites. To obtain a relative measure of the discouragement effect, I simply take the natural logarithm of each of the participation and unemployment rate variables in equation (3.3) above, and estimate the coefficients of the following equation:

$$\log(L/P) = \beta_0 + \beta_1 \log(\frac{L}{P})^i_{t-1} + \beta_2 \log(\frac{U}{L})^i_{t-1} + \beta_3 \text{TIME} \quad (3.4)$$
$$+ \beta_4 \text{TIME2} + v_t.$$

Table 3.1. Regression Results: Equation (3.3)
Dependent Variable = Monthly Labor Force Participation Rate

Independent Variable	Coefficient (t-Statistic) Blacks	Coefficient (t-Statistic) Whites
CONSTANT	27.2632*** (7.804)	42.7403*** (9.694)
$(L/P)_{t-1}$	0.5269*** (8.460)	0.3476*** (5.124)
$(U/L)_{t-1}$	-0.1474*** (-3.983)	-0.2832*** (-7.362)
TIME	-0.0350** (-2.361)	0.0822*** (7.917)
TIME2	0.0002*** (2.480)	-0.0005*** (-8.109)
R^2	.591	.847
D.W.	2.190	2.129

*** Significant at a 99 percent level of confidence or greater.
** Significant at a 95 percent level of confidence or greater.
* Significant at a 90 percent level of confidence or greater.

The coefficients β_1 and β_2 in this equation are approximately equal to the percentage change in the participation rate that arises from a 1 percent change in the lagged participation and unemployment rates, respectively, so that β_2 represents a relative measure of the strength of the discouraged worker effect. I estimate these coefficients using ordinary least squares and the same raw data used above. Estimates of the coefficients are presented by race in table 3.2. I have also conducted the analysis using the Cochrane-Orcutt technique to adjust for serial correlation. These results are presented in table 3.3. We see that for both sets of results, blacks exhibit a stronger discouraged worker response than do whites. According to table 3.3, a 1 percent increase in the unemployment rate causes an 11.8 percent decrease in participation for blacks, compared to a 5.6 percent decrease for whites. The effect is still statistically significant for both races.

Table 3.2. Regression Results: Equation (3.4)
Dependent Variable = Log of Monthly Labor Force
Participation Rate

	Coefficient (*t*-Statistic)	
Independent Variable	Blacks	Whites
CONSTANT	2.2261***	2.7900***
	(7.756)	(9.510)
$\log(L/P)_{t-1}$	0.5457***	0.3640***
	(8.964)	(5.407)
$\log(U/L)_{t-1}$	-0.1364***	-0.0727***
	(-4.158)	(-7.130)
TIME	-0.0007**	0.0013***
	(-1.971)	(7.735)
TIME2	0.000004**	-0.000008***
	(2.191)	(-7.929)
R^2	.604	.844
D.W.	2.117	2.193

*** Significant at a 99 percent level of confidence or greater.
 ** Significant at a 95 percent level of confidence or greater.
  * Significant at a 90 percent level of confidence or greater.

Table 3.3. Regression Results: Equation (3.4) Dependent Variable = Log of Monthly Labor Force Participation Rate

Independent Variable	Coefficient (*t*-Statistic) Blacks	Coefficient (*t*-Statistic) Whites
CONSTANT	1.8348*** (6.811)	2.0654*** (7.885)
$\log(L/P)_{t-1}$	0.6308*** (11.233)	0.5307*** (8.845)
$\log(U/L)_{t-1}$	-0.1181*** (-3.892)	-0.0560*** (-6.415)
TIME	-0.0005* (-1.836)	0.0010*** (6.561)
TIME2	0.000003** (2.112)	-0.000006*** (-6.724)
R^2	.756	.983
D.W.	2.023	2.092

*** Significant at a 99 percent level of confidence or greater.
** Significant at a 95 percent level of confidence or greater.
* Significant at a 90 percent level of confidence or greater.

An Analysis of Lagged Effects

There certainly is no reason to assume that the effect on participation of a change in measured unemployment is felt "instantaneously." Instead, the effect of a decrease in the unemployment rate today may be felt two, three, or six months, or even a year or two, from now. Further, the "structure" of this lag may differ by race. For instance, blacks may exhibit a strong immediate response, only to have the effect die out in a month or two so that the "total" effect is not as large as that for whites who have a weak immediate response, but also one that grows or lasts a very long time. To the extent that it is important to measure the "total" discouragement response, and that blacks and whites differ in the timing or the duration of the response, then knowledge of the structure of the lags in the discouragement effect can be important in interpreting and comparing the results presented above. In this section I examine the structure of these lags and any such racial differences.

Note that this analysis can be important when comparing the results above with the Clark and Summers results. Their coefficient is the sum of eight lagged coefficients, while the coefficients presented in table 3.3 are for a one-period lag only. In particular, Clark and Summers estimate the parameters of the equation:

$$\ln(PR)_t = \beta_0 + \sum_{k=0}^{7} \phi_k UP_{t-k} + \beta_2 T + \beta_3 T67 + r_t, \tag{3.5}$$

by race, sex, and age, where UP is the 35- to 44-year-old male unemployment rate, T is time, and T67 is a time trend beginning in 1967. They then define $\gamma_{PR}^i = -\sum_{k=0}^{7} \phi_k$ as a measure of the cyclical responsiveness of the participation rate of the ith group. It is γ_{PR} that they presented as 2.03 and 2.38 for blacks and whites and it is γ_{PR} that I have taken to be a measure of the discouraged worker effect.

First-Order Effects

I begin the analysis by examining the effect that past deviations in unemployment have on current deviations in participation in the following equation:

$$\log(\frac{L}{P})_t = \beta_0 + \beta_1 \log(\frac{L}{P})_{t-1} + \beta_2 \log(\frac{U}{L})_{t-k} + \beta_3 TIME \tag{3.6}$$

$$+ \beta_4 TIME2 + v_t,$$

for $k=1,2,\ldots,24$,

where k is the number of months lag. I take β_2 to be a "first order" measure of the lagged discouragement effect. I estimate β_2, by race, for each value of k. The estimates are presented in table 3.4, for both races.

For white teens we see a negative effect through the seventeenth month, with the effect decreasing (in absolute value) almost linearly, and a positive effect thereafter. The magnitude of the effect decreases for blacks, also, though the decline is not a constant one. For blacks the discouragement seems to "end" (the sign becomes positive) after eighteen months.

Let us define the "total effect" of the unemployment variable, through lag k, to be the sum of the regression coefficients for lags 1 through k. These sums are presented in columns 2 and 4 of table 3.4. We see that the total effect for blacks always lies above (except in the last three months) and peaks later than that for whites. Note that this total effect measure may provide a guide to determining where to "end" the lag. The point where the total effect is maximized could be an appropriate choice. For whites this is, again, at seventeen months. For blacks, the total effect is greatest at eighteen months. We can argue, then,

Table 3.4. Coefficients and Sums of Coefficients: Equation (3.6)

	Blacks		Whites	
Lag	Coefficient (1)	Sum (2)	Coefficient (1)	Sum (2)
1	-0.1181	-0.1181	-0.0560	-0.0560
2	-0.0795	-0.1976	-0.0595	-0.1155
3	-0.0297	-0.2273	-0.0653	-0.1808
4	-0.0601	-0.2874	-0.0605	-0.2413
5	-0.0885	-0.3759	-0.0623	-0.3036
6	-0.0429	-0.4188	-0.0428	-0.3464
7	-0.0712	-0.4900	-0.0405	-0.3869
8	-0.0105	-0.5005	-0.0357	-0.4226
9	-0.0399	-0.5404	-0.0262	-0.4488
10	-0.0473	-0.5877	-0.0255	-0.4743
11	-0.0245	-0.6122	-0.0178	-0.4921
12	0.0185	-0.5937	-0.0161	-0.5082
13	-0.0264	-0.6201	-0.0165	-0.5247
14	-0.0114	-0.6315	-0.0025	-0.5272
15	-0.0061	-0.6376	-0.0052	-0.5324
16	-0.0126	-0.6502	-0.0032	-0.5356
17	-0.0211	-0.6713	-0.0003	-0.5359
18	-0.0130	-0.6843	0.0036	-0.5323
19	0.0356	-0.6487	0.0050	-0.5273
20	0.0017	-0.6470	0.0048	-0.5225
21	0.0339	-0.6131	0.0100	-0.5125
22	0.0751	-0.5380	0.0087	-0.5038
23	0.0459	-0.4921	0.0082	-0.4956
24	0.0534	-0.4387	0.0117	-0.4839

that the discouraged worker effect lasts, for blacks, about eighteen months, slightly longer than for whites.

Now define the "total discouragement effect" to be the sum of the month specific effects up to the point where the individual effects "end." The total discouragement effect for whites would be $-.5359$, the sum of the coefficients through the seventeenth lag. The corresponding values for blacks for lag lengths of seventeen and eighteen months are $-.6713$ and $-.6843$, respectively. The last characteristic of the structure of the lags that we will examine is the rate at which these total effects are approached.

Define the "percent of the total discouragement effect attained by lag month k" (PTE) to be the sum of the coefficients through lag month k divided by the total discouragement effect as defined above. These values are presented in table 3.5 for whites and blacks, where the total discouragement effect is determined at $k=17$ for whites and at $k=18$ for blacks. The value of PTE is almost always

Table 3.5. Percent of Total Discouragement Effect Attained: Equation (3.6)

Lag	Blacks	Whites
1	17.3	10.5
2	28.9	21.6
3	33.2	33.7
4	42.0	45.0
5	54.9	56.7
6	61.2	64.6
7	71.6	72.2
8	73.1	78.9
9	79.0	83.7
10	85.9	88.5
11	89.5	91.8
12	86.8	95.8
13	90.6	97.9
14	92.3	98.4
15	93.2	99.3
16	95.0	99.9
17	98.1	100.0
18	100.0	99.3
19	94.8	98.4
20	94.5	97.5
21	89.6	95.6
22	78.6	94.0
23	71.9	92.5
24	64.1	90.3

less for blacks than for whites, indicating that the black effect approaches its total at a "slower rate" than the white effect. For whites, more than 95 percent of the total discouragement effect is felt by the thirteenth month. For blacks, only 90 percent of the total effect is felt in the same period, and 95 percent is not felt until almost the sixteenth month.

It is possible that these results depend very much on the specification in equation (3.1). In the next section I present the analysis in the context of a "distributed lag" model of the lag structure, one more widely used and accepted in the economics literature, and one that we can use as a benchmark for evaluating the results above.

Distributed Effects

I will write the distributed lag model to be estimated as

$$\log(\frac{L}{P})_t = \beta_0 + \beta_1 \log(\frac{L}{P})_{t-1} + \sum_{i=0}^{k-1} \gamma_i \log(\frac{U}{L})_{t-1-i} + \beta_3 \text{TIME} \qquad (3.7)$$

$$+ \beta_4 \text{TIME2}.$$

I make the standard assumption that the γ_i follows a polynomial in k.[1] In particular, the results presented below are based on the assumption that

$$\gamma_i = \alpha_0 + \alpha_1 i + \alpha_2 i^2, \qquad (3.8)$$

or that

$$\log(\frac{L}{P})_t = \beta_0 + \beta_1 \log(\frac{L}{P})_{t-1} + \sum_{i=0}^{k-1} (\alpha_0 + \alpha_1 i + \alpha_2 i^2) \log(\frac{U}{L})_{t-1-i}, \qquad (3.9)$$

$$= \beta_0 + \beta_1 \log(\frac{L}{P})_{t-1} + \alpha_0 z_{0t} + \alpha_1 z_{1t} + \alpha_2 z_{2t},$$

where $z_{0t} = \sum_{i=0}^{k-1} \log(\frac{U}{L})_{t-1-i}$,

$z_{1t} = \sum_{i=0}^{k-1} i \log(\frac{U}{L})_{t-1-i}$,

and $z_{2t} = \sum_{i=0}^{k-1} i^2 \log(\frac{U}{L})_{t-1-i}$.

I estimate β_0, β_1 and the α's in equation (3.9), by race, using the Cochrane-Orcutt technique, and then calculate the γ_i's using equation (3.8). These results are presented below in table 3.6 for $k=13$, 18, and 24. The sums of the coefficients are presented in columns 2 and 4 of the table. Using the definitions from above, the PTE's are presented by race in table 3.7.

In general, the results presented here support those generated by the specification of equation (3.6). The discouragement effect is seen to "last longer" for blacks than for whites. The effect for whites lasts between five and twelve months; for blacks, between eight and fifteen months. The total effect is again seen to peak later for blacks. The "percent of total discouragement effect attained" variable is again seen to be lower throughout for blacks than for whites.

Clearly the regression specification used here is rather arbitrary, even if it is widely used. Indeed, it is well known that there is no "correct" specification for this distributed lag model, in terms of both the degree of the polynomial and

Table 3.6(a). Coefficients and Sums of Coefficients: Equation (3.7) ($k = 13$)

	Blacks		Whites	
Lag	Coefficient (1)	Sum (2)	Coefficient (1)	Sum (2)
1	-0.0692	-0.0692	-0.0381	-0.0381
2	-0.0619	-0.1311	-0.0267	-0.0648
3	-0.0548	-0.1859	-0.0170	-0.0818
4	-0.0478	-0.2337	-0.0091	-0.0909
5	-0.0409	-0.2746	-0.0030	-0.0939
6	-0.0343	-0.3089	0.0013	
7	-0.0277	-0.3366	0.0039	
8	-0.0214	-0.3580	0.0047	
9	-0.0151	-0.3731	0.0038	
10	-0.0091	-0.3822	0.0011	
11	-0.0032	-0.3854	-0.0032	
12	0.0025		-0.0094	
13	0.0081		-0.0174	

Table 3.6(b). Coefficients and Sums of Coefficients: Equation (3.7) ($k = 18$)

	Blacks		Whites	
Lag	Coefficient (1)	Sum (2)	Coefficient (1)	Sum (2)
1	-0.0296	-0.0296	-0.0361	-0.0361
2	-0.0241	-0.0537	-0.0290	-0.0651
3	-0.0191	-0.0728	-0.0225	-0.0876
4	-0.0146	-0.0874	-0.0168	-0.1044
5	-0.0106	-0.0980	-0.0118	-0.1162
6	-0.0071	-0.1051	-0.0076	-0.1238
7	-0.0041	-0.1092	-0.0040	-0.1278
8	-0.0017	-0.1109	-0.0012	-0.1290
9	0.0002		0.0008	
10	0.0016		0.0022	
11	0.0025		0.0029	
12	0.0029		0.0028	
13	0.0027		0.0020	
14	0.0021		0.0005	
15	0.0009		-0.0016	
16	-0.0006		-0.0045	
17	-0.0028		-0.0082	
18	-0.0055		-0.0126	

Table 3.6(c). Coefficients and Sums of Coefficients: Equation (3.7)
($k = 24$)

	Blacks		Whites	
Lag	Coefficient (1)	Sum (2)	Coefficient (1)	Sum (2)
1	-0.0107	-0.0107	-0.0194	-0.0194
2	-0.0107	-0.0214	-0.0168	-0.0362
3	-0.0106	-0.0320	-0.0144	-0.0506
4	-0.0104	-0.0424	-0.0122	-0.0628
5	-0.0101	-0.0525	-0.0102	-0.0730
6	-0.0097	-0.0622	0.0083	-0.0813
7	-0.0091	-0.0713	0.0066	-0.0879
8	-0.0085	-0.0798	0.0050	-0.0929
9	-0.0077	-0.0875	0.0036	-0.0965
10	-0.0069	-0.0944	0.0024	-0.0989
11	-0.0059	-0.1003	-0.0014	-0.1003
12	-0.0049	-0.1052	-0.0005	-0.1008
13	-0.0037	-0.1089	0.0001	
14	-0.0024	-0.1113	0.0007	
15	-0.0010	-0.1123	0.0011	
16	0.0004		0.0013	
17	0.0020		0.0014	
18	0.0037		0.0013	
19	0.0056		0.0010	
20	0.0075		0.0005	
21	0.0095		-0.0000	
22	0.0117		-0.0007	
23	0.0140		-0.0017	
24	0.0163		-0.0028	

the lag length k.[2] Various specifications of these parameters can yield a wide range of results. I should note further, though, that great pains have been taken to ensure that the qualitative nature of the results (in terms of the racial comparisons) is not dependent on the polynomial or lag specification. The same regressions were run for polynomials up through the sixth degree and for lags up to forty-eight months. The results presented here were chosen on the basis of a number of variables, including R^2, standard error of the regression, sum of squared residuals, and the results from the preceding section. I am confident that the conclusions do not depend on the specifications.

In sum, the conclusion that the labor force participation of black male teenagers is more cyclically responsive than that of their white counterparts is confirmed even after allowing for different lengths and structures of the lags in the response. In particular, there is little evidence that white teens suffer a larger "total discouraged worker effect" than do black teens.

Table 3.7. Percent of Total Discouragement Effect Attained: Equation (3.7)

	Blacks			Whites		
Lag	$K=13$	$K=18$	$K=24$	$K=13$	$K=18$	$K=24$
1	18.0	26.7	9.5	40.6	28.0	19.3
2	34.0	48.4	19.1	69.0	50.5	35.9
3	48.2	65.6	28.5	87.1	67.9	50.2
4	60.6	78.8	37.8	96.8	80.9	62.3
5	71.3	88.4	46.8	100.0	90.1	72.4
6	80.2	94.8	55.4		96.0	80.7
7	87.3	98.5	63.5		99.1	87.2
8	92.9	100.0	71.1		100.0	92.16
9	96.8		77.9			95.7
10	99.2		84.1			98.1
11	100.0		89.3			99.5
12			93.7			100.0
13			97.0			
14			99.1			
15			100.0			

On the Nature of the Differential Response

The labor market is in continual motion. Workers leave the labor force continuously. At the same time, other workers enter it. The levels of these flows into- and out-of-the-labor-force combine to determine the labor force participation rate at a point in time. Changes in the rates of flow over time are what generate changes in the participation rate. An increase in the rate at which individuals enter the labor force will increase the labor force participation rate. A decrease will have the opposite effect, as will an increase in the rate of exit.

The discouraged worker effect as defined above is therefore the result of an increase (as unemployment rates rise) in the rate at which individuals leave the labor force, or a decrease (as unemployment rates rise) in the rate of entry, or both. The primary goal of this section is to identify the flow that generates the racial differential in the discouraged worker effect. As unemployment rates rise, does the probability that a teenager will leave the labor force rise by more for blacks than it does for whites? Or does the probability of entering the labor force fall more for blacks? I begin the answer to these questions by describing in more detail the "flow approach" to labor market dynamics.

The Gross Flow Approach

Let us define an individual's labor market status as either in or out of the labor force. Denote each of these states as P and N (for "participant" and "nonparticipant"), respectively. Then we represent the flows of workers between these states in the time interval $[t-1, t]$ in the following way:

	P_t	N_t
P_{t-1}	PP	PN
N_{t-1}	NP	NN

where the symbols in the cells represent the number of people making the appropriate transition. The entry *PN* is the number of individuals who were in state *P* (in the labor force) at time $t-1$ who were in state *N* (out of the labor force) at time *t*. I will designate the probability of making such a transition in lower case letters. For example, $pn = PN/P_{t-1}$ is the probability of making the transition from in the labor force to out of the labor force in the specified time interval. The relevance of these flow probabilities or "transition rates" lies in the fact that they determine the numbers of people in each of the states *P* and *N* at a point in time and, therefore, the labor force participation rate. This relationship can be expressed fairly simply. Define the "steady state" to be represented by the condition that the number of people leaving the participation state *P* must equal the number entering it, or $\alpha N = \beta P$, where $\alpha = np$ and $\beta = pn$. Then the steady state labor force participation rate, $r = P/(N + P)$, can be expressed as

$$r = \frac{\alpha}{\alpha + \beta}. \qquad (3.10)$$

Changes or differences in participation rates can therefore be linked to changes or differences in α and β, the transition probabilities. For instance, if white youth have a higher probability of making the *N* to *P* transition (α), then, *ceteris paribus*, they will have higher labor force participation rates. Likewise, if the probability α decreases when unemployment rates rise, then the participation rate will also decrease.

By definition, a person is a labor force participant whether working (employed) or not working but seeking employment (unemployed). The state *P* then comprises two distinct states, call them *E* and *U*. In the context of this three-state definition of the labor market we can now describe the complete set of labor market flows by the transition matrix

$$\begin{bmatrix} ee & eu & en \\ ue & uu & un \\ ne & nu & nn \end{bmatrix}$$

where ue, for instance, is the probability of making the transition from unemployment to employment. Using the definition of "steady state" from above, the participation rate, $r = P/(N + P)$, can now be written as

$$r = \frac{(\frac{a}{b}) + (\frac{c}{d})}{1 + (\frac{a}{b}) + (\frac{c}{d})}, \qquad (3.11)$$

where $a = ne + (\frac{ue \cdot nu}{ue + un})$

$b = en + (\frac{un \cdot eu}{un + ue})$

$c = nu + (\frac{eu \cdot ne}{eu + en})$

and $d = un + (\frac{ue \cdot en}{eu + en})$

Just as in the two-state case, given the transition rates, we can determine the steady state labor force participation rate. Consequently, changes in transition rates in response to changes in employment opportunities (or any other factor) can, through equation (3.11), be directly related to changes in participation rates.

To examine these relationships, we totally differentiate (3.11) and ask, How does an increase in the transition rate between states i and j affect, *ceteris paribus*, the participation rate? The results of that exercise are summarized in the first two columns of figure 3.1. In the first column is the transition rate change. The effects on the steady state participation rate of an increase in each rate, holding the other rates constant, are presented in the second column. Increases in the N to U and N to E transition rates increase the labor force participation rate. Increases in the U to N and E to N rates decrease it. The effects of increases in the U to E and E to U transition rates are in general ambiguous and depend on the relative magnitudes of the other rates. The entries presented in the figure for those rates are based on the true relationships presented in the following empirical analysis.

Now the discouraged worker effect is represented by a decrease in participation in response to an increase in the unemployment rate. That means that a decrease in the N to U transition rate in response to an increase in the unemployment rate would contribute to the discouraged worker effect. The relationships like that one, between the transition rates and the unemployment rate, which ensure that we observe the discouraged worker effect are presented in the third column of exhibit 3.1. If each of these relationships held as unemployment rates rose, then we would unambiguously observe the discouraged worker effect. In

Figure 3.1. Relationships between Transition Rates and Participation

Increase Transition from	Effect on Participation	Response to an Increase in Unemployment Necessary for Discouragement
N to U	Increase	Decrease
N to E	Increase	Decrease
U to N	Decrease	Increase
U to E	Increase	Decrease
E to N	Decrease	Increase
E to U	Decrease	Increase

the next section we test to see if these relationships do hold, and if any of them differ by race.

Empirical Analysis

I estimate the effects of employment opportunities on the levels of transition rates from the following regression equation:

$$\log(\lambda_{ij})_t = \beta_0 + \beta_1 \log(\text{URATE})_t + \beta_2 (\text{TIME})_t \qquad (3.12)$$
$$+ \Gamma(\text{monthly dummies}) + u_t,$$

where the variables are defined as follows. The transition probability (λ_{ij}) is defined to be the number of people that moved from state i to state j in the time interval ($t-1$, t), divided by the number of people in state i in month $t-1$. The data is from unpublished "Gross Change" tabulations from the Current Population Survey (CPS). Gross change (or "gross flow") data are the compilation of month-to-month changes in the labor force status of respondents to the CPS who are in the sample for any pair of consecutive months. Though a cross-sectional survey, the design of the CPS is such that in any pair of consecutive months, three-fourths of all households will be common. The data has not been published on a regular basis since 1952, when a number of technical problems became apparent. The three major problems, sample bias, response variability, and rotation group bias, are not important when used in the kind of analysis done here, however.[3] The data used is for the January 1972 to December 1981 period.[4] The mean values of the transition rate variables for the sample period are presented in table 3.8.

Table 3.8. Mean Values of Monthly Transition Probabilities: Male Teenagers, 1972–81

	Percent Making Transition	
Transition	Black	White
EN	13.67	9.25
UN	34.67	26.69
NE	6.7	12.72
NU	8.47	7.03
EU	7.04	4.23
UE	16.95	30.27

Referring to the table, we see that black youth were more likely than whites to make the *EN, UN, NU,* and *EU* transitions, and less likely to make the *NE* and *UE* transitions. As figure 3.1 indicates, these differences represent the "source" of the lower participation rates of black youth.

I use two definitions for the employment opportunities variable (URATE) in the regression analysis. First, I use the time contemporaneous own-race, own-age unemployment rate. The sample bias problem noted by Tella therefore should be mitigated here. Second, I use the time contemporaneous prime-age male unemployment rate, to make the analysis comparable to the work of Clark and Summers. The variable TIME takes the value 1 in January 1972. The gross flow data is not seasonally adjusted, so monthly dummy variables are also included in the regressions.

The estimates of β_0, β_1 and β_2 are presented in table 3.9 below, by race and by definition of the URATE variable. Referring to the table, we see that increases in the unemployment rate lead to the discouraged worker effect, for both races, primarily through its effects on the *N* to *E*, *U* to *E*, and *E* to *U* transition rates. An increase in unemployment rates decreases the probability of making transitions into the employment state, while it increases the probability of making the transition from employment to unemployment. For blacks, a decline in aggregate demand leads to discouragement also through its effect on the *U* to *N* transition rate. An increase in URATE corresponds with an increase in the *U* to *N* transition rate for blacks. The *U* to *N* transition, of course, is the one most similar to people's perceptions of the discouraged worker effect.

Note that the equations with the different definitions of URATE consistently produce the same signs on the estimated URATE coefficient, except in the case of the E to N transition rate. When the age/race specific rate is used (table 3.9(a)), we see that increases in the unemployment rate cause increases in the E to N transition rate, which is consistent with the discouraged worker effect. When the prime-aged male unemployment rate is used (table 3.9(b)), we see the opposite effect. Note also, however, that none of the estimates are significantly different from zero.

Regarding the racial difference in the strength of the discouraged worker effect, the results suggest that it is due to the following factors:

(1) As unemployment rates rise, black teens become more likely to make the transition from unemployment to out-of-the-labor-force. White teens become less likely.
(2) As unemployment rates rise, both black and white teens become less likely to make the transition from out-of-the-labor-force to employment. The effect is much larger for blacks, however.
(3) As unemployment rates rise, both black and white teens become less likely to move from unemployment to employment, and more likely to move from employment to unemployment. The magnitudes of these effects does not seem to differ significantly by race. But because the level of the U to N transition rate is higher for blacks than for whites (table 3.8), the combined effect is that a greater number, and a higher proportion, of black workers will leave the labor force as unemployment rates rise than will white workers.

These factors all combine to ensure that the decline in labor force participation due to an increase in unemployment, and hence the discouraged worker effect, is greater for blacks than for whites.

Table 3.9(a). Regression Results: Equation (3.12)
(URATE = Contemporaneous Rate)

Blacks

	EN	EU	UE	UN	NE	NU
CONSTANT	2.008**	-.828	6.206**	3.413**	3.995**	-.752
URATE	.112	.763**	-.973**	.003	-.654**	.780**
TIME	.001	-.002	-.002**	.001**	-.000	-.000
R^2	.656	.264	.554	.538	.819	.781
D.W.	2.006	1.910	1.985	2.006	1.979	1.988

Whites

	EN	EU	UE	UN	NE	NU
CONSTANT	-.159	2.047**	5.348**	3.824**	2.928**	.293
URATE	.585**	.068	-.780**	-.188**	-.321**	.556**
TIME	.001**	-.001**	.000	-.001**	.000	.001**
R^2	.689	.926	.821	.672	.951	.885
D.W.	2.008	2.035	2.015	1.963	1.994	1.938

**Significant at the 95 percent level of confidence or greater.

Table 3.9(b). Regression Results: Equation (3.12)
(URATE = Prime-Aged Male Rate)

Blacks

	EN	EU	UE	UN	NE	NU
CONSTANT	2.536**	1.813**	3.173**	3.316**	2.067**	1.865**
URATE	-.108	.002	-.310**	.096*	-.308**	.081
TIME	.002**	-.000	-.003**	.001	-.001	.001
R^2	.659	.225	.508	.549	.837	.755
D.W.	2.007	1.929	1.988	2.006	1.974	1.979

Whites

	EN	EU	UE	UN	NE	NU
CONSTANT	2.228**	1.077**	3.771**	3.433**	2.296**	1.435**
URATE	-.003	.273**	-.431**	-.092**	-.192**	.290
TIME	-.001**	.001	.001**	-.001	.000	.001**
R^2	.926	.639	.801	.666	.953	.879
D.W.	2.039	1.985	1.996	1.966	1.999	1.971

**Significant at the 95 percent level of confidence or greater.
*Significant at the 90 percent level of confidence or greater.

Summary and Concluding Remarks

The analysis in this chapter has shown that the labor force participation rate of black teens is relatively more responsive to changes in aggregate demand than is the participation rate of white teens. Based on a time series analysis of male teenage participation and unemployment rates for the 1972–85 period, we find that a 1 percent increase in the black male teenage unemployment rate is associated with approximately a 12 percent decrease in the black male labor force participation rate. A 1 percent rise in the white unemployment rate causes only a 6 percent decrease in the participation of whites. Because the lag or duration of the response can differ by race, I also examine the hypothesis that whites exhibit a greater "total" discouragement response than blacks do. The results of that analysis lend little support to the hypothesis. A first look at the "nature" of the differential response suggests that racial differences in the effects of unemployment rates on the flows into employment from nonparticipation and the flows from unemployment to nonparticipation are particularly important sources. Also important is the fact that blacks on average have higher rates of flow from unemployment to nonparticipation, regardless of the level of aggregate demand.

No explanations for these phenomena have been offered in this chapter. Indeed, we have as yet to offer any model of the determinants of either levels or cyclic variations in transition rates, though we did discuss a simple model of participation. A more extensive model is presented in the next chapter, in the context of the gross flow approach presented above.

4

The Discouraged Worker Effect in a Dynamic Model of Labor Supply

This chapter presents a dynamic model of the labor supply decision based on the work of Mortensen and Neumann (1984). The model is extended to include the notion that the rate at which workers receive job offers is a function of the level of aggregate demand. The modification allows us to examine the effects of aggregate demand on the transition rates and hence its effects on labor force participation rates. We therefore can model explicitly the relationship between the discouraged worker effect and transition probabilities. The extension also allows us to examine the role that racial differences in job offer arrival rates plays in the differential discouragement effects.

Overview

This is the basic form of the model: There are three states of the world, employment, unemployment, and nonparticipation, which a worker can occupy at a point in time. What is modelled is the worker's choice among those states. At a point in time the worker is faced by some wage offer (which could, of course, be zero) and by some "value of leisure." He derives utility from the values of these variables. The utilities are state dependent, however. For example, in this study I assume that the worker derives utility from the wage offer only when employed (if unemployed or not-participating, the utility of the wage offer is zero), he gets utility from leisure only when unemployed or out-of-the-labor-force, and the utility of leisure is greatest when out-of-the-labor-force, since some leisure must be given up in order to search for work. Each state is said to have some "value" associated with it at a point in time, defined to be the expected discounted life-time utility of leisure and income. Given the wage-offer/value-of-leisure pair faced by the worker, the worker is assumed to choose to occupy the state which yields the greatest value.

Over time the optimal state may vary, however, for the wage offers and values of leisure are assumed to change periodically to some other values, drawn from known distributions. When this occurs, there has been the "arrival of new information." I assume that this information also is state dependent. In particular, if the worker is in the employed state, I assume that he or she does not receive any wage offers from outside the firm, and that the wage offers made within the firm are either the current wage (which offers no "new information") or a zero wage (which can signify firing or layoff). Any new information received by employed workers is therefore assumed to consist only of zero wage offers. The new information for unemployed or nonparticipating workers consists of the new wage or value of leisure drawn. When new information does arrive, the worker is assumed to choose to occupy that state which yields the greatest value.

Clearly, if the wage offer and value-of-leisure faced by a worker never changed then the worker would never make any labor market transitions. Indeed, no one would ever be unemployed. The only reason that the unemployed state is ever preferred to the nonparticipation state is that unemployment (labor market search) may have the effect of changing the wage offer faced by the worker; the goal of search is to receive some other, better, wage offer. In general, in this model a necessary condition for a labor market transition to occur is a change in either the wage offer or the value of leisure faced by the worker.[1]

A basic assumption of the model is that these changes occur randomly. That is, the time until a new wage offer or value of leisure arrives is a random variable. The worker faces some wage offer at a point in time, for instance, from some known wage offer distribution, and he can expect a new wage offer to arrive at a point in the future, but he does not know how long that will be. The rate that the wage offer/value of leisure pair changes, the "arrival rate" of new information, is therefore an important characteristic of the worker's state. It is also instrumental in determining the probability that a worker will make a transition from one state to another. If the expected time until arrival of new information in a given state is infinity (i.e., the arrival rate is zero) then the probability that a worker will leave that state is zero.

We saw that transition probabilities differ according to race. Clearly this could be due to racial differences in the rate of arrival of new information. If the job offer arrival rate in the unemployment state is higher for white teens than for black teens, for instance, then *ceteris paribus* we should expect white teens to be more likely than black teens to make transitions from unemployment to employment. But the arrival of new information is only a necessary, not a sufficient, condition for a labor market transition. An unemployed worker may receive a new wage offer only slightly higher than his last offer and still choose to decline the offer and remain unemployed. Not only must a new wage (job) offer arrive, but that offer must be sufficiently different from the old one to induce the worker to change states. This second element is what Mortensen and Neumann call the "choice" component of the model, compared to the "chance" element represented by the information arrival rates. Policy makers should have obvious interest in determining the relative contributions of each of these components to differences across workers in transition probabilities. Do comparable black and white teens exhibit different participation rate behavior because blacks are more likely than whites to decline a given wage offer? Or do blacks simply receive fewer job offers than comparable whites due, say, to racial discrimination? The answers to these questions have important policy implications.

The primary goal in this chapter, however, is to identify sources of differences across workers in changes in transition rates associated with changes in the level of aggregate demand. To do so, I assume that the level of aggregate economic activity affects the information arrival rates. In particular, I assume that when aggregate demand is high, unemployed workers and non-participants receive more wage offers per period than when aggregate demand is low. This is equivalent to saying that the rate of arrival of wage offers varies directly with the level of aggregate demand. Consequently, the rate of arrival of new information also varies directly with aggregate demand. For *employed* workers I assume that the probability of being laid off is lower when aggregate demand is high than when it is low. That is to say that the rate of arrival of new information varies inversely with the level of aggregate demand for employed workers. These assumptions define the only ways that aggregate demand will affect participation rates in this model and so represent the sources of the discouraged worker effect. A major goal of this chapter is to determine the extent to which it is also the source of the racial differences in discouragement.

I should note that the *distributions* of wage offers and values of leisure are assumed to be constant over the business cycle. The worker draws from the same wage offer distribution in both good and bad times; only the frequency of draws of new information changes. I also assume that the worker does not detect trends or patterns in the information arrival rates. Consequently, a worker does not expect that the information arrival rate will be higher or lower tomorrow than it is today; rather, the worker expects tomorrow's arrival rate to be the same as today's. The worker's perception that "things will be better (or worse) tomorrow" is not a part of the model as I present it here. The effect of a change in aggregate demand on today's transition and participation rates is felt only through its effects on current information arrival rates. The discouraged worker effect is therefore very narrowly defined here.

Even so, the predictions of the model regarding the effects of changes in aggregate demand on transition rates are not clear cut. A major source of ambiguity lies in the fact that workers are allowed to receive new information in all states. Consider the case where both individuals that are unemployed and those that are out-of-the-labor-force receive wage offers. Assume that the rate of arrival of information is higher for unemployed workers, for there must be some return to search. Now suppose a worker is currently faced by a wage offer and value of leisure pair, such that given his expected probability of finding another offer if he searches, he prefers to be a nonparticipant and remain out of the labor force. Suppose that tomorrow he is faced by a higher probability of receiving a new wage offer, in both the unemployed and not-participating states, because of a rise in aggregate demand. Our question is, Will he be as likely to remain out-of-the-labor-force tomorrow as he is today? The expected return to search has risen, raising the "value" of the unemployment state, which should induce the worker to enter the labor force. But the value of nonparticipation has risen also, for the probability that the worker receives a wage offer in that state has risen also. The effect on flows between unemployment and nonparticipation depends on the magnitudes of the changes in the values of the states. That is, is the rise in the return to search greater than or less than the rise in the return to nonparticipation? The answer to that question will be seen to depend on a number of factors, including the worker's costs of search and preferences, in addition to the relative magnitudes of the changes in the arrival rates. This implies that the responsiveness of transition rates (and therefore participation rates) to changes in aggregate demand also depends on costs of search and the relative magnitudes of the changes in arrival rates, which suggests that observed differences in the discouraged worker effect need not be attributed to differences in "behavior." Each of these ideas is developed in more detail below.

The balance of the chapter begins with a presentation of the model, its relation to transition probabilities, and its relation to the discouraged worker phenomenon. I then present the conditions necessary to unambiguously observe the discouraged worker effect, and discuss the likelihood that the conditions can be met. Finally, I discuss the implications of the model for examining the causes of the racial differential in discouragement.

The Model

Denote the three states of the labor market as E, U, and N, for employed, unemployed, and not-participating, respectively.[2] At a point in time, the worker occupies one of those states, and derives utility from the wage he earns if employed, $y = w + e_1$, and his value of nonmarket time (leisure), $u = v + e_2$, where w is his mean expected wage, v is his mean expected value of leisure, and e_1 and e_2 are random disturbances. A hypothetical relationship between y, w, and e_1 is depicted in figure 4.1. A similar relationship exists for u, v, and e_2. Write the currently realized wage offer/value of nonmarket time pair, $(y, u) = (w + e_1, v + e_2)$, as $(x + e)$ and define the utility associated with that pair as $U_i(x + e)$. Note that U depends on the state occupied, i. In general, U also depends on the worker's personal characteristics, such as education, age, family size, sex, or race. These variables also play important roles in the determination of the wages offered to individual workers (e.g., blacks may receive lower wage offers than do whites) and the values they assign to leisure.

Figure 4.1. The Relationship between y, w, and e_1

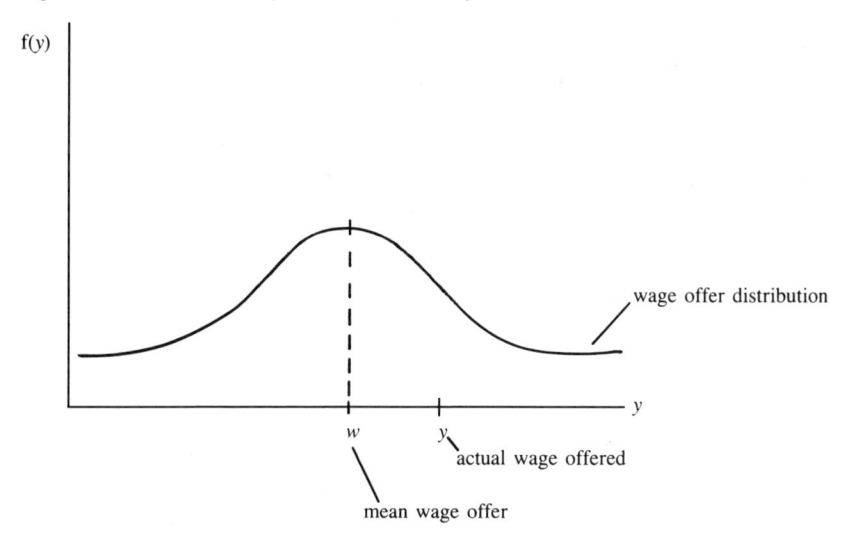

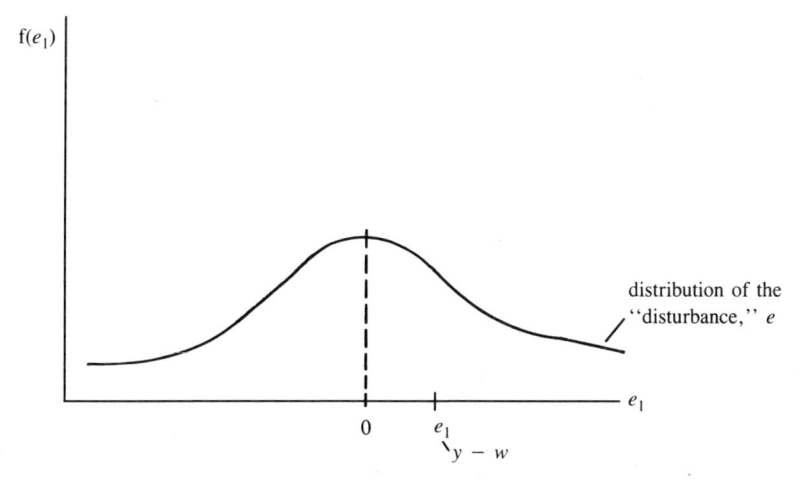

wage offer distribution

mean wage offer

actual wage offered

distribution of the "disturbance," e

Assume that e changes from time to time to some value $\tilde{e}$ at random intervals. For instance, the worker may draw a new wage, y, and $\tilde{e}_1$ is the difference between that new wage and the mean wage, w. The change in the disturbance is therefore $\tilde{e}_1 - e_1$. Let $F_i(\tilde{e}, e)$ be the distribution of the new disturbance $\tilde{e}$ given the current value, e.[3] The worker is assumed to assess his state occupancy each time he is faced by a new disturbance $\tilde{e}$, choosing the state that yields the highest level of discounted future utility. The disturbance is assumed to changes

68   Dynamic Model

at some rate $\eta_i(x,z)$, I assume that the random time until arrival of new information has a negative exponential distribution, such that the expected time before e changes again is $1/\eta_i(x,z)$. The arrival rate is dependent on the worker's wage and value-of-leisure characteristics x, the state i, and some index of aggregate employment opportunities, z. Examples of the variable "z" could be the inverse of the aggregate unemployment rate, or the level of GNP.

We can write the expected present value of future utility associated with state i as a function $V_i(x,e,z)$ of the current disturbance, the worker's stationary wage and value-of-leisure pair, and the index of employment opportunities. The value associated with state i today is the expected utility derived while currently in state i, plus the expected value of the state the worker chooses to occupy if and when new information arrives. This sum can be written as

$$V_i(x,e,z) = E\{\int_0^{t_i} U_i(x+e) e^{-\rho s} ds + e^{-\rho t_i} \max_k V_k(x,e,z) | e\}$$

where t_i is the time of arrival of new information, and ρ is the discount rate. The first term can be interpreted as the expected utility enjoyed in state i prior to the arrival of new information. The second term represents the expected present value of the optimal state choice after a new wage offer, value-of-leisure pair has arrived. When the new disturbance e is realized, the worker chooses the state k which yields the greatest expected value. Note that if new information never arrives, then $t_i = $ infinity, and the value of the state is defined to be the utility of the current wage offer/value of nonmarket time pair, appropriately discounted. Taking expectations, the equation can be written as

$$V_i(x,e,z) = \frac{u_i(x+e)}{\rho + \eta_i(x,z)} + \frac{\eta_i(x,z)}{\rho + \eta_i(x,z)} \int \max_k V_k(e,x,z) \, dF_i(\tilde{e},e). \quad (4.1)$$

Now let

$$A_j(x,z) = \{e | V_j(e,x,z) = \max_k V_k(e,x,z)\} \quad (4.2)$$

be the set of disturbances $e = (e_1, e_2)$ such that state j is preferred to the other states (i.e., the value associated with state j, given the disturbance e, is at least as large as the value in any other state). If any wage offer/value of leisure pair in the set e is faced, then the worker will choose to occupy state j. These disturbances e are said to be "in the acceptance set A_j." An example of the acceptance sets A_E, A_N, and A_U is presented in figure 4.2. Referring to the figure, relatively high values of nonmarket time (e_2) are seen to make the worker prefer leisure. Relatively high values of wages (e_1) are associated with employment. The worker is in the unemployment state only when the values of both are relatively low.[4] A worker moves from one state to another only when a value of e_1 or e_2

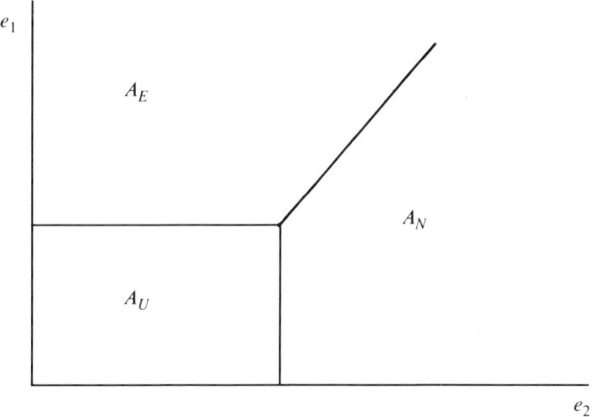

Figure 4.2. The Employment, Unemployment, and Not-Participating Acceptance Sets

arrives which is in some other acceptance set. Define the probability that the next disturbance $\tilde{e}$ falls in the acceptance set $A_j(x,z)$ as

$$\pi_{ij}(e,x,z) = \int_{A_j(x,z)} d F_i(\tilde{e},e). \tag{4.3}$$

This is just the probability that state j will be preferred at the next change in e, given that we are now in state i. I refer to this probability as "the choice probability π_{ij}."

Now the probability of a transition from state i to state j, the transition rate λ_{ij} in chapter 3, is the product of the arrival rate and (4.3), or

$$\lambda_{ij}(x,e,z) = \eta_i(x,z) \pi_{ij}(e,x,z). \tag{4.4}$$

That is, the probability of a transition from state i to state j is the product of the rate at which the disturbances "e" change when in state i, and the probability that some other state j will be preferred, given a change in the disturbance. From equation (4.4), we see that workers that have high arrival rates will be more likely to make transitions than those with low arrival rates. Also, workers with "larger" acceptance sets A_j will be more likely to make transitions into state j than will other workers.

The effect of the index of aggregate demand, z, on the probability of a transition from state i to j can be found by differentiating (4.4), yielding

$$\frac{\delta \lambda_{ij}}{\delta z} = (\frac{\delta \eta_i}{\delta z}) \pi_{ij} + (\frac{\delta \pi_{ij}}{\delta z}) \eta_i. \tag{4.5}$$

70   Dynamic Model

I will assume throughout this chapter that $\delta\eta_U/\delta z > 0$, $\delta\eta_N/\delta z > 0$, and $\delta\eta_E/\delta z < 0$ (note that π_{ij} and η_i are by definition greater than or equal to zero). As described above, these assumptions imply that the arrival rate of information (e.g., job offers) increases with z in the unemployed and out-of-the-labor-force states, while the rate of arrival of information (e.g., layoffs) decreases with z for employed workers. It is clear from equation (4.5) and these assumptions that the effects of z on the transition rates are not unambiguous. For instance, a rise in aggregate demand can cause a decrease in the N to U transition rate if $\delta\pi_{NU}/\delta z$ is negative. On the other hand, $\delta\lambda_{NU}/\delta z$ is positive if $\delta\pi_{NU}/\delta z$ is positive. The directions of the effects of z on transition probabilities therefore depend critically on the directions and magnitudes of the effects of z on the choice probabilities.

Our goal is to identify the effect of aggregate demand on labor force participation rates—the discouraged worker effect. To do so we must examine the effects that the various transition rates have on participation. Recall that the participation rate varies directly with the N to U, N to E, and U to E transition probabilities, and that it varies inversely with the probabilities of transitions from U to N, E to N, and E to U. Then if the N to U, N to E, and the U to E transition rates vary directly with aggregate demand, and the U to N, E to N, and E to U transition rates move in the opposite direction, we will observe the discouraged worker effect in this model. Consequently, each of the following conditions will contribute to measured discouragement:

$$\delta\lambda_{NU}/\delta z > 0,\ \delta\lambda_{NE}/\delta z > 0,\ \delta\lambda_{UE}/\delta z > 0,$$

and

$$\delta\lambda_{UN}/\delta z < 0,\ \delta\lambda_{EN}/\delta z < 0,\ \delta\lambda_{EU}/\delta z < 0.$$

From equation (4.5), our assumptions, and these inequalities, we can determine the relationships between the choice probabilities π_{ij} and the index of aggregate demand, z, which will generate the discouraged worker effect, by identifying the conditions that ensure that the inequalities above hold. Indeed, equation (4.5) implies:

(a) $\dfrac{\delta\lambda_{NU}}{\delta z} > 0 \quad \text{if } \dfrac{\delta\pi_{NU}}{\delta z} > 0,$

(b) $\dfrac{\delta\lambda_{EN}}{\delta z} < 0 \quad \text{if } \dfrac{\delta\pi_{EN}}{\delta z} < 0,$

(c) $\dfrac{\delta\lambda_{NE}}{\delta z} > 0 \quad \text{if } \dfrac{\delta\pi_{NE}}{\delta z} > 0,$

(d) $\dfrac{\delta \lambda_{EU}}{\delta z} < 0$ if $\dfrac{\delta \pi_{EU}}{\delta z} < 0,$

(e) $\dfrac{\delta \lambda_{UE}}{\delta z} > 0$ if $\dfrac{\delta \pi_{UE}}{\delta z} > 0,$

and (f) $\dfrac{\delta \lambda_{UN}}{\delta z} < 0$ if and only if $\dfrac{\delta \pi_{UN}}{\delta z} < 0.$

If the inequalities in (a) through (f) are satisfied, then we will unambiguously observe the discouraged worker effect. Conditions (a) and (c) require that a rise in aggregate demand increases the probability that workers will choose to leave the nonparticipation state and enter the labor force, given an arrival of new information. A fall in the level of aggregate demand must have the opposite effect. Conditions (b) and (f) require that a rise in aggregate demand is associated with a decrease in the probability that workers will choose to leave the labor force at the next information arrival date. Each of these seems consistent with the standard notion of the relationship between participation and aggregate demand. Conditions (d) and (e) imply that the worker must be more likely to prefer employment to unemployment as aggregate demand rises. This condition seems counterintuitive, for an increase in the arrival rate of information to unemployed workers is likely to increase the returns to search enough that their reservation wages rise, which would tend to decrease the transitions into employment.

Effects of Changes in Employment Opportunities

In this section I examine the ways that employment opportunities, as measured by the index of aggregate demand, z, affect the six transition probabilities, λ_{ij}. Of primary concern is the relationship between π_{ij} and z. From equation (4.3) we see that the choice probabilities depend critically on the "sizes" of the acceptance sets A_j. The probability that the next wage offer faced by a worker is in his acceptance set A_E depends on the size of the set of acceptable wage offers. We therefore can identify the effects of changes in employment opportunities on choice probabilities by identifying the effects of employment opportunities on the acceptance sets A_j.

Using equation (4.1), for an (x,z) pair we can find the (e_1,e_2) pairs such that workers are indifferent between the three labor market states. These pairs define the boundaries of the acceptance sets A_E, A_N, and A_U. Note that finding the value of e_1 that makes the worker indifferent between the Employment and Unemployment states is equivalent, in the language of the job search literature, to finding the worker's "reservation wage." If we assume (1) that wage offers are enjoyed only when employed and (2) that leisure is enjoyed only when out of the labor

72 Dynamic Model

force, which implies (3) that the information arrival rate must be higher when searching than when out of the labor force (otherwise no one would be unemployed), then it can be shown[5] that the slope of the boundary between A_E and A_N is positive, between A_E and A_U is zero, and between A_U and A_N is infinite. Those are the boundaries depicted in figure 4.2. The question that we ask is, How do changes in the rates of arrival of information affect these boundaries? Because we are interested in the discouraged worker effect, we are particularly interested in the conditions under which a rise in the index of aggregate demand, z, causes a decrease in the probability that the next value e_1 or e_2 faced by the worker will be in the acceptance set A_N. That probability decreases with z only if the "size" of the set A_N decreases with z. The goal here is to derive the conditions under which that result holds.

Effects of Z on A_N

Note that the boundary of the set A_N is defined by

$$V_N(e,x,z) = \max[V_E(e,x,z), V_U(e,x,z)]. \tag{4.6}$$

Holding e_1 constant, differentiation of this condition yields

$$\frac{\delta e_2}{\delta z} = \frac{\dfrac{\delta[\max(V_E,V_U) - V_N]}{\delta z}}{\dfrac{\delta[V_N - \max(V_E,V_U)]}{\delta e_2}}. \tag{4.7}$$

To ensure that the set $A_N(x,z)$ decreases with z, we need $\delta e_2/\delta z > 0$. Graphically, this means that the boundary $V_N = \max(V_N,V_E)$ has shifted to the right; that is, given a value for e_1, the value of e_2 that solves equation (4.6) increases with z. This is depicted in figure 4.3.

Now by the assumptions above, the denominator in (4.7) is positive, such that $\delta e_2/\delta z > 0$ if and only if

$$\frac{\delta \max(V_E,V_U)}{\delta z} > \frac{\delta V_N}{\delta z}. \tag{4.8}$$

That is, $A_N(x,z)$ decreases with z if and only if the effect of z on the value of the next best alternative E or U is greater than the effect of z on the value of nonparticipation. If the values of the various states all rise as a result of an increase in z, and they rise by the same amount, then the boundaries between the acceptance sets will not shift, and x will have no effect on the choice probabilities π_{ij}.

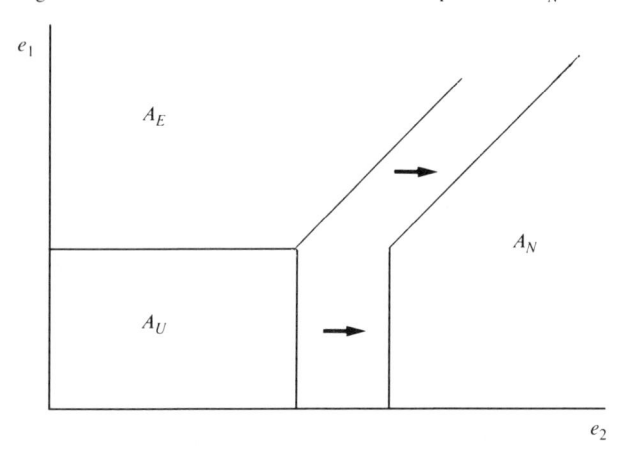

Figure 4.3. A Decrease in the Size of the Acceptance Set A_N

Defining π_j to be the probability that state j is preferred at the next arrival of information, regardless of the initial state, then equations (4.7) and (4.8) imply that $\delta\pi_N/\delta z < 0$ if and only if

$$\frac{\delta(V_N - V_E)}{\delta z} < 0 \quad \text{when } V_N = V_E > V_U \tag{4.9a}$$

$$\frac{\delta(V_N - V_U)}{\delta z} < 0 \quad \text{when } V_N = V_U > V_E. \tag{4.9b}$$

These conditions are sufficient to ensure that transition rates from the labor force to nonparticipation states should decline with increases in z, and that flows into the labor force should increase. These of course are characteristics of the discouraged worker effects.

We need to examine equation (4.1) to determine how restrictive conditions (4.9a) and (4.9b) are. To simplify the analysis, I will assume that the utility functions have the following forms: $U_E(\cdot) = y$, $U_N(\cdot) = u$, and $U_U(\cdot) = u - c$, where y is the actual wage earned if employed, u is the utility of leisure, and c is some cost associated with search. Second, assume that the disturbance $\tilde{e}$ is independent of the state occupied, or $F_i(\cdot) = F(\cdot)$. Now write (4.1) as

$$V_i(x,e,z) = \frac{U_i(\cdot)}{\rho + \eta_i(x,z)} + \frac{\eta_i(x,z)}{\rho + \eta_i(x,z)} \psi(x,e,z), \tag{4.10}$$

where $\psi(x,e,z) = \int \max_k V_k(e,x,z) \, dF(\tilde{e},e)$.

74 Dynamic Model

Then the difference between the values of the not-participating and the unemployment states is

$$(V_N - V_U) = \frac{u}{\rho + \eta_N(\cdot)} - \frac{u - c}{\rho + \eta_U(\cdot)} \qquad (4.11)$$

$$+ \psi \left[\frac{\eta_N(\cdot)}{\rho + \eta_N(\cdot)} - \frac{\eta_U(\cdot)}{\rho + \eta_U(\cdot)} \right]$$

$$= 0 \text{ on the boundary.}$$

Note that if the arrival rates in the two states are the same (i.e., $\eta_N = \eta_U$), then the difference between the two value functions would always be positive, such that workers would never prefer searching for work to being out-of-the-labor-force. Workers would therefore never be unemployed. The acceptance sets for such a case are depicted in figure 4.4. Workers will prefer unemployment only when the arrival rate in the unemployment state is sufficiently large relative to the arrival rate for nonparticipants.

Figure 4.4. The Acceptance Sets with No Unemployment

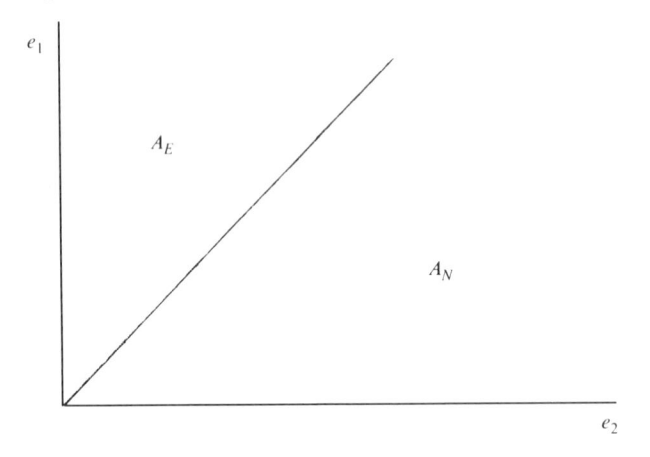

Differentiating (4.11) with respect to z and e_2, holding e_1 constant, yields that $\delta(V_N - V_U)/\delta z < 0$ if and only if

$$\left(\frac{\delta \eta_N}{\delta z}\right) \left[\frac{\rho \psi - u}{(\rho + \eta_N)^2}\right] - \left(\frac{\delta \eta_U}{\delta z}\right) \left[\frac{\rho \psi - u + c}{(\rho + \eta_U)^2}\right] \qquad (4.12)$$

$$+ \psi'(z) \left[\frac{\eta_N}{\rho + \eta_N} - \frac{\eta_U}{\rho + \eta_U}\right] < 0.$$

Condition (4.9a) is satisfied only when the inequality in (4.12) is satisfied. Consequently, equation (4.12) is a necessary condition for us to observe the boundary between A_N and A_U shift to the right as z increases.

The condition regarding the boundary between A_N and A_E is that $\delta(V_N - V_E)/\delta z < 0$ if and only if

$$\left(\frac{\delta\eta_N}{\delta z}\right)\left[\frac{\rho\psi - u}{(\rho + \eta_N)^2}\right] - \left(\frac{\delta\eta_E}{\delta z}\right)\left[\frac{\rho\psi - y}{(\rho + \eta_E)^2}\right] \quad (4.13)$$

$$+ \psi'(z)\left(\frac{\eta_N}{\rho + \eta_N} - \frac{\eta_E}{\rho + \eta_E}\right) < 0.$$

Both equations (4.12) and (4.13) must hold in order to get the discouraged worker effect in terms of transitions between the nonparticipation state N and the participation states E and U.

Recall that we assumed $\eta_U > \eta_N$, $\delta\eta_N/\delta z > 0$, $\delta\eta_U/ > 0$, and $\delta\eta_E/\delta z < 0$ above. These assumptions imply that a sufficient condition for equation (4.12) to hold is

$$\left(\frac{\delta\eta_U}{\delta z}\right)\left[\frac{\rho\psi - u + c}{(\rho + \eta_U)^2}\right] > \left(\frac{\delta\eta_N}{\delta z}\right)\left[\frac{\rho\psi - u}{(\rho + \eta_N)^2}\right]. \quad (4.14)$$

Note that, *ceteris paribus*, condition (4.14) will be "more likely to hold" (a) the greater the responsiveness of the arrival rate to changes in z when searching, (b) the less the responsiveness of the arrival rate when not searching, and (c) the greater the cost of search, c. That means that the boundary between the A_N and A_U acceptance sets is more likely to shift in response to a change in aggregate demand if the worker has, for instance, high costs of search. Note also that the levels of the arrival rates affect the probability that condition (4.14) will be met. Workers with relatively high arrival rates in the unemployment state are seen to be less likely to exhibit "discouraged worker" behavior. The same can be said for those with relatively low arrival rates in the out-of-the-labor-force state.

A necessary condition for the inequality in equation (4.13) to hold is $\eta_N < \eta_E$. That is, a rise in the level of aggregate demand will generate an increase in the probability that workers will move from N to E (and a decrease in the probability of moves from E to N) only if the arrival rate of information is higher in the employment state than in the nonparticipation state. An increase in z increases the value of employment, since the expected value of earnings rises due to a lower probability of layoff. But an increase in z also increases the value of nonparticipation since nonparticipants face an increased probability of receiving a job offer. The extent of these changes seems to depend on the initial levels of the arrival rates. Since $\delta\eta_E/\delta z < 0$ and $\delta\eta_N/\delta z > 0$, there will in general exist some value of z such that $\eta_E = \eta_N$, and the inequality in equation (4.13) will not hold. We therefore cannot in general determine the effect of changes in aggregate demand on the worker's choice between the E and N states. Consequently, it is possible that an increase in aggregate demand could generate a shift to the right in the $V_N = V_U$ boundary and at the same time generate a shift to the left in $V_N = V_E$. This is depicted in figure 4.5. The result is that the "size" of the acceptance set A_N could remain unchanged. Therefore, we cannot determine the sign of $\delta\pi_N/\delta z$.

Figure 4.5. A Shift in the Boundary $V_N = V_U$ Accompanied by a Shift in $V_N = V_E$

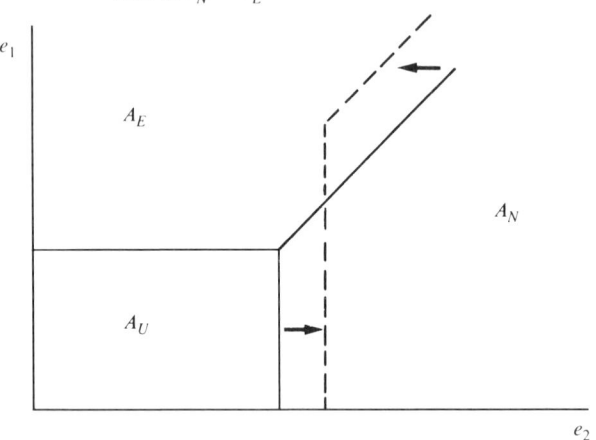

I should note that the model above is a very general one and encompasses many of the standard models of the discouraged worker effect which do not yield ambiguous results. Most models examine the decision being made by a worker who does not receive job offers if he does not search, and they ignore the effects that aggregate demand has on employed workers. In essence, they consider the model above when $\eta_N = 0$, $\delta\eta_N/\delta z = 0$, $\eta_E = 0$ and $\delta\eta_E/\delta z = 0$. The value functions then reduce to

$$V_N = \frac{u}{\rho}$$

$$V_E = \frac{y}{\rho}$$

and

$$V_U = \frac{u - c}{\rho + \eta_N} + \frac{\eta_N}{\rho + \eta_N}\psi,$$

such that

$$\frac{\delta(V_N - V_E)}{\delta z} = 0$$

and

$$\frac{\delta(V_N - V_U)}{\delta z} > 0$$

when

$$-(\frac{\delta\eta_U}{\delta z})[\frac{\rho\psi - u + c}{(\rho + \eta_U)^2}] - \psi'(z)[\frac{\eta_U}{\rho + \eta_U}] < 0.$$

Under our assumptions, this last condition will always hold. Therefore, we unambiguously observe that increases in aggregate demand induce workers from nonparticipation into the labor force, choices which are consistent with the discouraged worker phenomenon. The ambiguities in the more general model arise because workers are allowed to receive new information in each and every state, and the information arrival rates in every state are allowed to depend on z.

Effects of Z on A_E

From figure 3.1 we saw that the labor force participation rate will fall if the U to E transition rate falls or the E to U transition rate rises. This is because the two result in more people being in the unemployment state than would be otherwise and consequently, given a U to N transition rate, we observe more people leaving the labor force. If this occurs as aggregate demand falls then we call it an increase in discouragement. The effects of aggregate demand on λ_{EU} and λ_{UE} are therefore relevant to our discussion. Recall from conditions (d) and (e) above that sufficient conditions for λ_{EU} to fall and λ_{UE} to rise as z rises are $\delta\pi_{EU}/\delta z < 0$ and $\delta\pi_{UE}/\delta z > 0$. In this section I present conditions under which conditions (d) and (e) are met.

The boundary of the set A_E in figure 4.2 is given by

$$V_E(x,e,z) = \max[V_U(x,e,z), V_N(x,e,z)].$$

Holding e_2 constant and differentiating, we have

$$\frac{\delta e_1}{\delta z} = \frac{\frac{\delta(\max(V_N, V_U) - V_E)}{\delta z}}{\frac{\delta(V_E - \max(V_N, V_U))}{\delta z}}. \tag{4.15}$$

78 Dynamic Model

By our assumptions the denominator in (4.15) is positive, such that the acceptance set A_E increases with z, or $\delta e_1/\delta z < 0$, if and only if

$$\frac{\delta(\max(V_N, V_U))}{\delta z} < \frac{\delta V_E}{\delta z}. \qquad (4.16)$$

Equivalently, $\delta \pi_E/\delta z > 0$ if and only if

$$\frac{\delta(V_E - V_N)}{\delta z} > 0 \quad \text{when } V_E = V_N > V_U, \qquad (4.17a)$$

$$\frac{\delta(V_E - V_U)}{\delta z} > 0 \quad \text{when } V_E = V_U > V_N, \qquad (4.17b)$$

If these conditions are met, then a rise in aggregate demand will generate the change in the acceptance sets depicted in figure 4.6.

Figure 4.6. An Increase in the Acceptance Set A_E

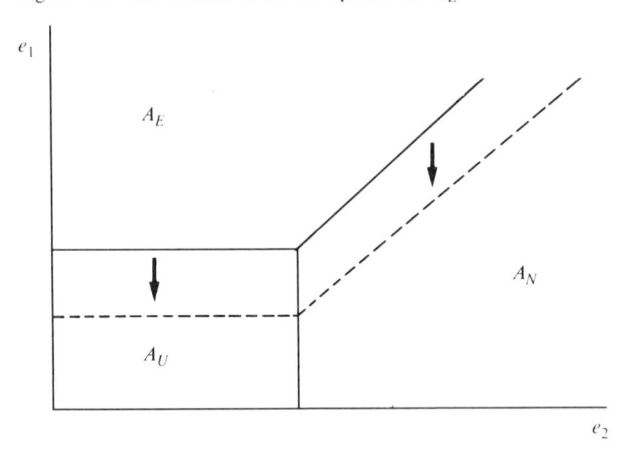

Because condition (4.17a) is the opposite of condition (4.9a), we know from above that a sufficient condition for (4.17a) to hold is $\eta_E \leq \eta_N$. The necessary condition for (4.17b) is

$$(\frac{\delta \eta_E}{\delta z}) [\frac{\rho \psi - U_E}{(\rho + \eta_E)^2}] - (\frac{\delta \eta_U}{\delta z}) [\frac{\rho \psi - U_U}{(\rho + \eta_U)^2}]$$

$$+ \psi'(z)(\frac{\eta_E}{\rho + \eta_E} - \frac{\eta_U}{\rho + \eta_U}) > 0.$$

Given our assumptions, this implies that η_E must be greater than η_U. A sufficient condition for (4.17b) to be violated, therefore, is $\eta_U \geq \eta_E$. Again, because $\delta\eta_E/\delta z < 0$ and $\delta\eta_U/\delta z > 0$, there exists some z such that $\eta_E = \eta_U$ and the condition will not hold. In general, then, we cannot determine the sign of $\delta\pi_E/\delta z$. More important, we cannot unambiguously sign $\delta\pi_{EU}/\delta z$ and $\delta\pi_{UE}/\delta z$, which are necessary to ensure that conditions (d) and (e) above hold.

Summary

The model indicates that changes in employment opportunities generally have ambiguous effects on transition rates between labor market states. The sources of the ambiguities are twofold. First, from equation (4.5), the total effect of a change in z is the sum of the "direct" effect of z on the rate of arrival of new information and the "indirect" effect of z on the choice probability. This indirect effect is felt through the effects of aggregate demand on the acceptance sets A_j. The sign of the total effect depends on the signs and magnitudes of these two effects. The signs of the effects on the choice probabilities are therefore critical determinants of the sign of the total effect.

The second source of ambiguity comes from the choice probabilities themselves. In order to eliminate the ambiguity, we must place restrictions on both the relative levels and rates of change of the information arrival rates. These restrictions can take many forms, but in general we can argue that the probability that a worker will exhibit discouraged worker behavior is higher if the response of the arrival rate of information in the unemployment state is large relative to the response of the arrival rate in the nonparticipation state, if the costs of search are high, if the arrival rate of information in the unemployed state is small, and if the arrival rate in the not-participating state is large.

As a final note, recall that I have been concentrating primarily on the effects of aggregate demand through its effects on the arrival rates of job offers. In fact, aggregate demand can affect transition rates in other ways, especially through its effects on the levels of wage offers made by firms and on the value of nonmarket time. In general, those factors that decrease the levels of the wage offers of firms should increase the probability of making the U to N transition because the returns to search have declined. Likewise, employed workers will be less likely to quit work to search for another job and unemployed workers will be less likely to accept jobs so that the E to U and U to E rates should decline. Individuals not in the labor force will also see lower returns, so that the N to U and N to E transition rates should also decline.[6] Factors that increase the value of nonmarket activity should decrease the rate of flow out of nonparticipation and increase the rates of flow into it. Examples are the birth of a child or some windfall profit or inheritance. Because some factors that increase the value of nonmarket activity can also be seen to subsidize search (e.g., the windfall pro-

80 Dynamic Model

fits, or wealth in general), their total effect on the N to U and U to N transition rates will be ambiguous. The U to E transition rate, however, would be expected to decline. Certainly each of these factors is important when discussing the effects of aggregate demand on participation. As aggregate demand rises, for instance, we might expect the mean wage offer to shift upward, or even the variance of the wage offer distribution to change. As aggregate demand falls, the mean wage offer may fall. In addition, as aggregate demand falls a worker's nonlabor income may change due to the unemployment of a spouse, or in our case, the unemployment of a mother or father. I have ignored these factors and their effects. Note, however, that the first effect is not important for our discussion if the wages of teenagers are fairly rigid over the business cycle. This is probably true. There is evidence that teens' wages are more rigid than are those of adults.[7] The minimum wage certainly provides some downward rigidity. It can be argued that the minimum makes teens' wages relatively sticky upward, also.[8] Nevertheless, I will attempt to account for the effects of the wage and wealth variables in the empirical analysis.

Differences in Discouragement across Workers

The fact that black teenagers exhibit a stronger discouraged worker response than do whites could be the result of some of the sources of differentials in choice probabilities. I will make some general statements about the sources of differentials in the responsiveness of transition probabilities.

Refer again to equation (4.5), which presented the change in transition probability λ_{ij} due to a change in z as a function of the information arrival rate η_i, the responsiveness of the arrival rate, $\delta\eta_i/\delta z$, the choice probability π_{ij}, and the responsiveness of the choice probability, $\delta\pi_{ij}/\delta z$. The most obvious sources of racial differences in $\delta\lambda_{ij}/\delta z$ are in this equation. If $\delta\pi_{ij}/\delta z$ is greater (in absolute value) for whites than for blacks, for instance, then $\delta\lambda_{ij}/\delta z$ will be greater for whites than for blacks also. The factors that affect the responsiveness of the choice probabilities noted above then also contribute to the responsiveness of the transition probability. Ignoring the fact that $\delta\pi_{ij}/\delta z$ may depend on $\delta\eta_i/\delta z$, then we also know that if $\delta\eta_i/\delta z$ is greater for blacks than for whites then $\delta\lambda_{ij}/\delta z$ should also be greater for blacks than for whites. The effects of differences in π_{ij} and η_i, however, depend on the states occupied and on the direction of the response of the choice probabilities. If in the employment state, then $\delta\eta_E/\delta z$ is negative and the effect of a higher choice probability is a lower response in the transition rate. If in either of the other two states, the effect is a higher transition rate response. Even this conclusion is not straightforward, however, for the effect of a change in z on the choice probability may depend on the level of the choice probability. A change in aggregate demand may have less an (absolute) effect on the choice probability if the choice probability is very high, for instance. In that case, the sign of the effect of the level of the choice probability on the transition rate can be ambiguous. The effect of the level of the information arrival rate is also in general ambiguous.

Still, we can derive some statements about racial differences in the responsiveness of transition rates from our general model, though not very powerful ones. For example, our results suggest that the more pronounced decline (as unemployment rates rise) in the N to E transition rate for blacks could be due to a more pronounced decline for blacks in the arrival rate of information to workers out of the labor force. But we cannot theoretically preclude the hypothesis that the responsiveness of the arrival rates is in fact the same for blacks and whites and that the source of the differential is instead that blacks are less likely than whites to accept the job offers that do arrive. Because the sources of differences across workers in the responsiveness of transition rates are so many, their identification and relative importance becomes more an empirical rather than a theoretical issue. However, we can conclude the following: workers will exhibit differential participation rate behavior as a result of differences in the value of leisure, differences in the costs of search, differences in the wages they can expect to receive if employed, and differences in the responsiveness of the arrival rates of information to changes in aggregate demand. All of these factors can combine to generate the racial differences in the discouraged worker effect. That is, if black youth have higher values of leisure than white youth, or if they have higher costs of search, or if their job offer probabilities decrease by more in an economic downturn, then we should expect a more pronounced discouraged worker effect.

One final source of differences, but one which has been ignored in the model presented here, lies in workers' abilities to interpret, recognize, or assimilate the information that they do receive. If blacks and whites receive information at the same rate, but they assimilate that information differently or do not interpret it as the same, then they may exhibit differential participation rate responses to changes in aggregate demand.[9] This may be an important point and should be kept in mind when interpreting the empirical results presented in the next chapter.

5

Parameter Estimates from the Seattle Income Maintenance Experiments

This chapter presents the results of an analysis of data from the Seattle Income Maintenance Experiments. The primary goal is to examine the effects of aggregate demand, as measured by the unemployment rate, on the probabilities of making labor market transitions. This analysis differs from the analysis in chapter 3 in that the data set is for a cross-section of individual black and white youth, and thus allows us to control for individual variations in age, education, nonlabor income, and expected wages. An additional contribution of the analysis is its attempt to differentiate between the sources of transitions resulting from differences in choice probabilities and those resulting from differences in information arrival rates, following the work of Mortensen and Neumann (1984).

The Statistical Framework

This analysis requires that we express flow probabilities as functions of individual specific and other variables, hereafter referred to as "transition functions." I estimate the parameters of those functions with a maximum likelihood estimator.[1] The specification of the likelihood function is such that "right-censored spells," spells which are not completed by the end of the sample period, are appropriately dealt with. "Left-censored spells," spells which begin the sample time-period and may not be observed in their entirety or may be preceded by unobserved spells, have been ignored in this study. Because we are examining teenagers, for whom the first spell in our sample *is* often the actual, entire first spell, then the initial conditions problem may not be that important. For the sample used here, more than 42 percent of the youth were 18 years old or younger at the beginning of the observation period. A little more than 38 percent were out-of-the-labor-force at the beginning of the experiments, and probably had not had any previous labor market experience.[2]

Many parameterizations of the transition function have been used in the job search, worker-firm matching, and labor turnover literature. These include the exponential function (Tuma and Robbins, 1980; Lundburg, 1981, 1984; Burdett et al., 1981; Mortensen and Neumann, 1984; Kiefer, 1985), the Weibull function with both time-stationary and time-varying parameters (Weiner, 1982), and a very general specification which includes all of these as special cases, used by Flinn and Heckman (1980, 1982). I use both the Weibull function and the exponential in this analysis, with time-stationary parameters.

The Weibull specification of the transition function is

$$h_{ij}(t) = e^{X\beta_{ij}} t^{\gamma_{ij}}, \tag{5.1}$$

where X is a vector of exogenous variables, the values of which are assumed constant over the duration of a spell, β and γ are vectors of coefficients, t is the length of time in the spell, and $h_{ij}(t)$ is the transition function, conditioned on the length of time in the state. If $\gamma = 0$, then the specification reduces to the exponential. Either specification assures that $h_{ij}(t)$ is nonnegative, a desirable property. The advantage of the Weibull specification over the exponential is that the Weibull allows for various models of "duration dependence." That is, with the Weibull specification the hazard function is allowed to depend on the length of time in the state. If the coefficient γ is greater than zero then the hazard increases with duration. We might expect this to occur for transitions from unemployment to out-of-the-labor-force, for instance, in accordance with the conventional notion of the discouraged worker effect. The exponential function implies that the transition function is constant over time ($\gamma = 0$). One problem with the Weibull specification, however, is that the duration dependence is assumed to be monotone. A generalization of the specification to allow the possibility that the hazard function may increase and then decrease over time (or vice versa) is an important topic for further research. The specification used by Flinn and Heckman (1980, 1982) allows for such forms of duration dependence.

The Data

The data is derived from the public use files for the control group of the Seattle and Denver Income Maintenance Experiments.[3] The experiments, which began in 1970 in Seattle and 1971 in Denver, were designed to facilitate research on the effects of income transfers on work effort. In Seattle, 2,042 families were enrolled in the program. A little less than half of the families acted as a control group. The data files contain forty-eight months of data for each family, collected in three- to five-month intervals.

The particular data set used here was constructed from the original public use files and was provided to me in the following form:[4] each observation consists of the length of time that was spent in a particular state, the calendar time at which the spell in that state began, an index of the next state occupied, and a set of individual and family specific characteristics, defined as of the beginning of the spell. These include the respondent's age, level of education (grades completed), predicted real hourly earnings, and the amount of money received by his family from various income transfer programs (the control group did not participate in any of the experimental programs, but they were allowed to participate in any existing programs). These include AFDC payments, listed as a separate variable, and a variable for other public transfers (PUBTRN) which is the sum of SSI, general assistance, social security, veterans and survivors payments, training stipends, the GI Bill, and the net value of food stamps purchased. See Lundberg (1981) for a detailed description of the construction of these variables. Important variables that are *not* provided concern the individual's marital status and other family responsibilities (e.g., number of children, if any). "Children" variables do exist, but they are for the family as a whole rather than for the individual teen. Whether the teenager is a parent or not should be a factor related to labor force behavior, but that data is not available. The sample means for the variables that *are* used in this analysis are presented in table 5.1, for the entire sample, by race, and by spell. Note that the EDUCATION variable is defined only for the beginning of the experiment, another major deficiency of the data set. Had school enrollment status been continuously recorded for the respondents

Table 5.1(a). Means of Selected Variables
(All Spells)

	Entire Sample	Blacks	Whites
EDUCATION (highest grade at the beginning of experiment)	11.05	11.06	11.05
AGE (beginning of experiment)	18.80	18.67	18.93
AGE (beginning of spell)	19.23	19.10	19.35
WAGE	$ 2.30	$ 2.08	$ 2.46
AFDC	$44.71	$59.46	$32.23
PUBTRN	$41.08	$37.92	$43.78
% BLACK	46.60	—	—
Total number of spells	339	158	181
Number of individuals	76	36	40

Table 5.1(b). Means of Selected Variables

(Employment Spells)

	Entire Sample	Blacks	Whites
AGE	19.38	19.17	19.53
WAGE	$ 2.41	$ 2.19	$ 2.55
AFDC	$41.83	$62.30	$28.55
PUBTRN	$40.90	$39.34	$41.92
% BLACK	39.85	—	—
Number of spells	133	53	80

(Unemployment Spells)

	Entire Sample	Blacks	Whites
AGE	19.31	19.20	19.42
WAGE	$ 2.15	$ 2.07	$ 2.21
AFDC	$47.25	$64.67	$31.47
PUBTRN	$42.95	$45.71	$40.41
% BLACK	48.80	—	—
Number of spells	125	61	64

(Nonparticipation Spells)

	Entire Sample	Blacks	Whites
AGE	18.86	18.89	18.84
WAGE	$ 2.10	$ 1.69	$ 2.59
AFDC	$45.45	$48.61	$41.74
PUBTRN	$38.39	$25.17	$53.89
% BLACK	54.32	—	—
Number of spells	81	44	37

I could have constructed a better years of school variable, but that information is not available. Some other problems with the data are that the youth are a little older than I would like (ranging in age from 15 to 21), and the sample size is small (only seventy-six individuals). The sample size is not too serious a problem, however, because the unit of observation is the spell, of which there are more than 300. Far more observations would be available if we included the teens from the Denver Experiments, but variations in the unemployment rate in Denver were so small during the sample period that analysis of that data would be fruitless.

Referring again to table 5.1, the means for the other variables indicate that the whites were a little bit older than the blacks, they could expect higher wages, and they received substantially less in AFDC payments, but slightly more in other transfers. Most of these racial differences also exist by spell, except that nonparticipating blacks are as old as their white counterparts. Comparing the means across spells, we see that the average age is greatest for those people in the employment state, followed by unemployment and nonparticipation, as might be expected. The predicted wage variable also is greatest in employment and followed by unemployment and nonparticipation, at least for blacks. The income transfers are each greatest for individuals in the unemployment state.

The "employment opportunities" variable used in this analysis is the monthly civilian unemployment rate (URATE), for all workers in the Seattle-Everett SMSA, averaged over the duration of each spell. The rate ranged from a minimum of 6.2 percent in January of 1970 to a maximum of 13.5 percent in July of 1971.

Reduced Form Estimates

In this section I present estimates of the parameters of the transition function specified in equation (5.1) above. The likelihood function is maximized with respect to the β_{ij}'s and γ, using a Newton-Raphson convergence algorithm described in Weiner (1982). I present results using two specifications of the vector X. First, X consists of the variables EDUCATION, AGE, URATE, LNWAGE, AFDC, and PUBTRN, where LNWAGE is the natural logarithm of the expected wage. The estimation was done by race and for the sample as a whole. When the entire sample is used, X also includes a dummy variable indicating the race of the respondent (BLACK), and the interaction variable BLACK*URATE, used to examine racial differences in the effect of the unemployment rate variable. The second specification includes all of these variables and adds three more interaction variables. Recall that the model presented in chapter 4 predicts that the effects (on transition rates) of changes in aggregate demand may vary according to an individual's wage, value of leisure, or costs of search. I examine these hypotheses by including variables which account for interactions between URATE and WAGE, AFDC, and PUBTRN. With regard to the AFDC and PUBTRN interactions, the belief is that AFDC and PUBTRN affect a workers value of leisure and/or costs of search (they can subsidize search).

Predictions regarding the effects of these and the other variables are sometimes ambiguous. The EDUCATION, AGE, AFDC, and PUBTRN variables are all used to measure differences in the value of leisure and costs of search. Older, more educated workers may place less value on leisure. At the same time they may be more attractive to employers. We would therefore expect EDUCATION or AGE to decrease flows out of employment and increase flows into employment and out of non-participation. Given a level of education, however, increased AGE may signal that the teenager is not a good student and lead to a decrease in the demand for his labor. This latter effect would tend to decrease transitions into employment so that the net effect of AGE is ambiguous. The AFDC and PUBTRN variables are thought increase the value of leisure and subsidize search, so that we would expect them to be positively related to transitions from E to U and E to N and negatively related to transitions from U to E and N to E. The effect of the WAGE variable has received much empirical attention in studies of other age groups (Burdett et al., 1981; Mortensen and Neumann, 1984). Burdett, Mortensen, Kiefer, and Neumann show that, in a general model of the type presented in chapter 4, the effects of the wage are in general ambiguous. But if we assume that information arrival rates are independent of the wage then we can predict that λ_{UE} and λ_{NE} are increasing functions of the wage rate, while λ_{EN} and λ_{UN} are decreasing functions of the wage.

The maximum likelihood estimates are presented in table 5.2. The results in column (1) are for the specification that does not include the additional interaction terms. Referring first to the results for the entire sample, we see that increases in the unemployment rate are associated with significant increases in the transition rates from E to U and N to U, and decreases in the transition rates from U to E and N to E. These results are generally consistent with those reported in chapter 3, and all lead to the discouraged worker effect. Some of the results *by race* are different from those found in chapter 3, however. In particular, the unemployment rate has no significant effect on the U to E transition rate for blacks. In addition, the sign has changed (that is, increases in URATE lead to *increases* in λ_{UE}). Further, increases in URATE are found to increase the N to E transition rate for whites. For the other transitions, the results are pretty much the same as those in chapter 3. The effect of URATE on λ_{EU} and λ_{EN} are greater (in absolute terms) for blacks than for whites, and both effects contribute to a stronger discouraged worker effect for blacks. The racial difference in the effect on λ_{NU} also contributes to the differential discouraged worker effect (i.e., increases in URATE increase λ_{NU} for whites but decrease λ_{NU} for blacks).

The effects of the other variables are generally as predicted above. Increased levels of AFDC payments tend to increase transitions from both U to N and N to U. But because the effects are of roughly the same magnitude, there may be little total effect on participation. Note, however, that the AFDC effects are stronger for blacks. Other public transfers (PUBTRN) seem to decrease the U to E transition rate, especially for whites, though the magnitude of the effect is less the greater the URATE. The effect of the WAGE variable is as predicted in many cases, though the direction of the effect often depends on whether the WAGE*URATE interaction variable is included. WAGE has the predicted signs for the U to E, N to E, and U to N transition rates, in all cases and for blacks and whites, when no URATE interaction is used. But the signs change for the N to E and U to N transitions when the interactions are included. The results for the race dummy variable indicate that there are racial differences in the E to N and U to E transition rates that are unexplained by the variables used here.

The one variable that significantly affects *all* the transition probabilities is the length of time in the state, though there are some racial differences in the magnitudes of the effects. The estimates of γ for the sample as a whole indicate that there is negative duration dependence for the E to U and E to N transitions (i.e., the probability that a worker will leave employment declines the longer he has been employed), while there is positive duration dependence in the other states. The effects for the U to N and N to E transitions differ markedly by race. If we can interpret the effect of duration as a measure of true "discouragement," then the results for the U to N transition could indicate that white teenagers are actually much more easily discouraged than are blacks. Note that positive duration dependence for the N to E and N to U transitions is counter to previous findings for older workers (e.g., Weiner, 1982). I have no explanation for this result.

In sum, the results in table 5.2 suggest that contributors to racial differences in labor force participation may include racial differences in levels of employment opportunities, wages, AFDC payments, and other public transfer payments. Racial differences in the effects of some of these variables also contribute to differential levels of participation, particularly in the effect of AFDC on transitions from E to N and U to N. Still, there are some racial differences in transition probabilities that are not explained by these variables. The results in this section also indicate that some transition probabilities are very responsive to variations in unemployment rates, and that racial differences exist in some of the effects. The racial difference in the effect of the unemployment rate on the U to E transition rate found in the time series analysis of chapter 3 is not found here, however.

Table 5.2(a). Reduced Form Parameter Estimates
(Entire Sample)

	EU (1)	EU (2)	EN (1)	EN (2)	UE (1)	UE (2)	UN (1)	UN (2)	NE (1)	NE (2)	NU (1)	NU (2)
CONSTANT	-4.1893**	-.2499	1.4185	-.4169	-5.9274***	-6.3711*	-.6296	-3.5546	-6.9898***	-3.6339	-8.2921***	-5.0906*
EDUCATION	-.1523**	-.1635**	.1363	.1374	.1425**	.1553**	-.0554	-.0841	-.1188	-.0834	-.0991	-.0988
AGE	.0022	.0201	-.2993**	-.3116***	.1072*	.0506	-.0699	-.0605	.2228**	.2008*	.1347	.1116
URATE	.2298***	-.2002	.0032	.2040	-.2358***	-.0986	-.1214	.1695	.0274	-.3370*	.3387**	.0480
WAGE	.2078	-.5447	-.1505	.2731	.5181***	1.0879*	-.1799***	.7795*	.3372***	-.5066	-.0450	-1.2533***
AFDC	.0015	-.0054	.0009	.0182	.0004	-.0121	.0028**	-.0028	.0015	.0147	.0033***	-.0028
PUBTRN	-.0003	-.0046	.0014	-.0144	.0006	-.0418***	.0027**	.0050	-.0073*	-.0051	.0020	.0058
BLACK	-.3281	-.3647	-5.1182*	-5.8527*	-5.1064***	-4.9452***	1.3814	2.6195	-1.3262	-2.7032	3.1946	1.6113

WAGE* URATE		.0777		-.0410		-.0545	-.0921**	.0853**	.1154***
AFDC* URATE		.0006		-.0015		.0011	.0006	-.0013	.0006
PUBTRN* URATE		.0004		.0014		.0035***	-.0002	-.0002	-.0004
BLACK* URATE	.0491	.0555	.4528*	.5121*	.4027***	.3812***	-.0894	-.2048	.2372	-.3390*	-.1864
γ	-.2894***	-.2836***	-.2641***	-.2706***	.2035***	.2539***	.2799**	.2677*	.0805	.2887**	.3792***	.2624*	.3409***

***Significant at the 95 percent level of confidence.
**Significant at the 90 percent level of confidence.
*Significant at the 80 percent level of confidence.

Table 5.2(b). Reduced Form Parameter Estimates
(Blacks)

	EU (1)	EU (2)	EN (1)	EN (2)	UE (1)	UE (2)	UN (1)	UN (2)	NE (1)	NE (2)	NU (1)	NU (2)
CONSTANT	-1.8292	-.3723	-9.8120*	-9.1622	-8.4884***	-7.2976	-.2195	-2.410	-4.6899	-.5167	-3.2492	.0010
EDUCATION	-.2558***	-.2349**	.3906	.6226**	.1015	.0549	-.1778	-.1923*	.0875	.0805	-.1323	-.1807
AGE	-.0969	-.0153	-.1289	-.2953	.0203	.0331	.0369	.0294	.0164	.0165	.0592	.0421
URATE	.3034***	-.0160	.4570**	.4281	.1517	.0634	-.2243	.0228	-.0212	-.5317**	-.0176	-.3766*
WAGE	.1889	-.2918	-.1271	-.2178	.3723***	.6023	-.0207**	1.0109**	.2314***	-1.7153***	-.1207	-4.3282***
AFDC	.0003	-.0159	-.0002	.0863*	.0015	-.0115	.0034**	-.0049	.0023	.0108	.0045**	.0101
PUBTRN	.0022	-.0043	-.0020	-.6860*	.0011	-.0447	.0031**	.0032	-.0098	-.0020	.0053*	.0372***
WAGE* URATE		.0474		.0089		-.0212		-.1020**		.2050***		.4062***
AFDC* URATE		.0015		-.0073*		.0012		.0008		-.0004		.0000
PUBTRN* URATE		.0006		.0546*		.0038		.0000		-.0013		-.0045***
γ	-.1102	-.0896	-.3556***	-.3831***	.4077***	.4402***	.2081	.1972	.0627	.4092	.2539	.6723

***Significant at the 95 percent level of confidence.
**Significant at the 90 percent level of confidence.
*Significant at the 80 percent level of confidence.

Table 5.2(c). Reduced Form Parameter Estimates
(Whites)

	EU (1)	EU (2)	EN (1)	EN (2)	UE (1)	UE (2)	UN (1)	UN (2)	NE (1)	NE (2)	NU (1)	NU (2)
CONSTANT	-5.7186***	-3.6610	3.2261	1.8522	-7.7093***	-10.5260	13.1322	19.0228	-12.8374***	-24.5778***	-9.5059***	-10.0273**
EDUCATION	-.1039	-.1192	-.0374	-.0333	.0868	.1667*	-.6303	-.8668	-.3860***	-.5359***	-.0897	-.0993
AGE	.1276	.1207	-.3481**	-.3472**	.1294	.0109	-.4147	-.5484	.5250***	.8397***	.1847	.2126
URATE	.1920***	.0132	-.0194	.1268	-.2110***	.1943	-.2419	-.3356*	.1349	.8345***	.3390**	.3320
WAGE	.0212	-.3412	.0582	.2631	.8559***	1.9320	-1.0187***	-4.1266	.5951***	1.7796***	.0192	.5273
AFDC	.0044	.0093	.0028	.0190	-.0001	-.0133	.0069	.0103	.0040	.1432	.0031*	-.0078
PUBTRN	-.0027	-.0048	.0017	-.0055	.0008	-.0384**	-.0008	.0295	-.0042	.0999	.0013	-.0273*
WAGE* URATE		.0368		-.0230		-.1028		.2586		-.1163**		-.0482
AFDC* URATE		-.0004		-.0015		.0011		-.0003		-.0165		.0010
PUBTRN* URATE		.0002		.0007		.0033**		-.0023		-.0104		.0027*
γ	-.3564***	-.3539***	-.2114	-.2132	.1364	.1985*	1.4086***	1.6377***	.9272***	1.1968***	.3907***	.5003*

***Significant at the 95 percent level of confidence.
**Significant at the 90 percent level of confidence.
*Significant at the 80 percent level of confidence.

Structural Estimates

Though the results point to factors that help explain variations in labor force participation, they do not allow us to differentiate between alternative hypotheses regarding the relationships. We have found that an increase in aggregate demand leads to a decrease in the probability of a transition from unemployment to employment, but we do not know whether this is through the choice probabilities or through the information arrival rates. Mortensen and Neumann (1984) suggest that it is possible to distinguish between these two effects, using a method suggested by Olsen, Smith, and Farkas (1986).

To do so we need to make a few important assumptions. Recall that we can specify the transition rate between state i and j as

$$h_{ij}(x) = \eta_i(x)\pi_{ij}(x), \tag{5.2}$$

where x is a vector of individual specific characteristics, η_i is the arrival rate of new information in state i, and π_{ij} is the transition choice probability. If we assume that the transition rate can also be specified as an exponential function of x,

$$h_{ij} = e^{X\delta_{ij}}, \tag{5.3}$$

where δ_{ij} is a vector of parameters, then the "reduced form" parameters δ_{ij} can be expressed as

$$\delta_{ij} = \alpha_i + \beta_{ij}, \tag{5.4}$$

where α_i and β_{ij} are "structural" parameters from

$$\pi_{ij} = e^{X\beta_{ij}}/\sum_j e^{X\beta_{ij}} \tag{5.5}$$

and

$$\eta_i = e^{X\alpha_i}\sum_j e^{X\beta_{ij}}. \tag{5.6}$$

We can distinguish between the effect a variable has on the choice probability π_{ij} and the effect it has on the information arrival rate η_i by estimating α_i and β_{ij}.

It is not possible to estimate the parameters in this form, however, because the system is not identified.[5] Identification is possible, however, if we assume that $\pi_{ij}(x) = \pi_i(x)$, which implies $\beta_{ij} = \beta_i$ for all i and each j. Indeed, the system is then over-identified. This restriction supposes that the probability that the arrival of new information will induce a person to change states is independent of the state he currently occupies. In the notation of chapter 4, it is equivalent to assuming that $\tilde{e}$ is independent of e. Only the characteristics of the new state "matter."

The estimates of the parameters are presented in table 5.3, by race, but only for the specification of X which excludes the interaction terms. Again, we maximize the log likelihood function, but we now specify the transition function as $h_{ij} = e^{X(\alpha_i + \beta_j)}$. Because of over-identification, we can arbitrarily set one parameter vector equal to zero. Following Mortensen and Neumann, I have set $\beta_U = 0$.

The reported coefficients β_E^* and β_N^* are therefore to be interpreted relative to β_U. That is, $\beta_E^* = \beta_E - \beta_U$ and $\beta_N^* = \beta_N - \beta_U$.

The results suggest that the nature of the effects of the unemployment rate on transition rates differs by race. For blacks, an increase in the unemployment rate is only associated with an increase in the arrival of new information to the employment state (e.g., layoffs). The effect on the information arrival rates to unemployment and nonparticipation are of the correct sign, but they are not significantly different from zero. For whites, the unemployment rate affects both arrival rates *and* choice probabilities. An increase in the unemployment rate is seen to decrease whites' preferences for both employment and nonparticipation (relative

Table 5.3(a). Structural Parameter Estimates (Entire Sample)

	α_E	α_U	α_N	β_E^*	β_N^*
CONSTANT	-3.9263**	-7.1858***	-7.2228*	1.8399	7.2235***
EDUCATION	-.1497**	-.0522	-.1499*	.1464	.0663
AGE	-.0451	.1177	.1452*	-.0227	-.2247*
URATE	.2692*	.1302	.3026**	-.3147**	-.2383*
LNWAGE	.1664	.1957*	-.0312	.2991***	-.4514***
AFDC	.0023***	.0041***	.0033***	-.0037**	-.0014
PUBTRN	.0001	.0024*	.0009	-.0025*	.0007
BLACK	-2.0232	.7603	3.0158*	-4.2881**	-.3126
BLACK*URATE	.1925	-.0893	-.2984*	.3651*	.0596

ln $L = -1058.4$

***Significant at the 95 percent level of confidence.
**Significant at the 90 percent level of confidence.
*Significant at the 80 percent level of confidence.

Table 5.3(b). Structural Parameter Estimates
(Blacks)

	α_E	α_U	α_N	β_E^*	β_N^*
CONSTANT	-3.8834	-1.2119	-2.8955	-3.7778	-.2009
EDUCATION	-.2153**	-.3267*	-.1594	.3769**	.2051
AGE	-.0883	.0308	.0901	-.0645	.0147
URATE	.4280***	-.0092	-.0315	.0693	-.1301
LNWAGE	.1471	.2509*	.0089	.1138	-.3504***
AFDC	.0009	.0048*	.0042**	-.0042*	-.0013
PUBTRN	.0028*	.0083*	.0032	-.0084*	-.0051
ln L = -511.4					

***Significant at the 95 percent level of confidence.
**Significant at the 90 percent level of confidence.
*Significant at the 80 percent level of confidence.

Table 5.3(c). Structural Parameter Estimates
(Whites)

	α_E	α_U	α_N	β_E^*	β_N^*
CONSTANT	-5.2637**	-6.7314*	-7.4296***	-.1295	12.1101***
EDUCATION	-.1279	.1664	-.1503	-.0961	-.0665
AGE	.0676	-.0076	.1451	.1582	-.3894***
URATE	.2237***	.1204	.3463***	-.2968**	-.2345*
LNWAGE	.0413	.0149	-.1355	.6012***	-.5145***
AFDC	.0061***	.0006	.0022	-.0006	-.0025
PUBTRN	-.0017	.0018	.0002	-.0019	.0029*
ln L = -531.1					

***Significant at the 95 percent level of confidence.
**Significant at the 90 percent level of confidence.
*Significant at the 80 percent level of confidence.

to unemployment). The effect is insignificant for blacks. The BLACK*URATE coefficient η_N indicates that a racial difference also exists in the effect of URATE on the arrival of information to the workers who are out of the labor force. This could be a source of the differential in the discouraged worker effect.

The coefficients β_E for the BLACK variable and for the BLACK*URATE interaction variables suggest that the choice probability π_E is *greater* for blacks than for whites when URATE is above 11.6 percent. Because increases in URATE tend to *increase* π_E for blacks relative to whites, it is difficult to conclude that the choice probability is the source of the differential discouraged worker effect. But for values of URATE less than 11.6, it could be an important source of the difference in participation rate *levels,* through its effect on the N to E and U to E transition rates, which are significantly lower for blacks (see table 3.8). This racial difference could arise from a number of sources. I have argued that the notion that blacks have less work ethic or ambition should be rejected. Instead, the racial difference in the choice probability could arise from the greater propensity among blacks to be involved in nonmarket (illegal) activities which provide other sources of income, or from differences in the costs of search. It could also be the result of differences in the ability to assimilate job market information. The EDUCATION variable should account for some of those differences, however.

A racial difference also exists in the coefficient α_N. As indicated by the variable BLACK, the coefficient is significantly larger for blacks, though the difference decreases as the unemployment rate increases. Indeed, the estimates indicate that α_N is *smaller* for blacks than for whites for unemployment rates above 10.1 percent. Because the average value of URATE over the 1970-73 time period was 10.125 percent, then the racial difference is such that α_N is actually smaller rather than larger for blacks, though only slightly so. The results for the BLACK and BLACK*URATE variables for the α_U coefficient indicate that α_U is smaller for blacks than for whites for values of URATE greater than 8.5 percent.

The results for the WAGE variable indicate that higher expected wages increase preferences for employment relative to unemployment, and for unemployment relative to nonparticipation, as was found by Mortensen and Neumann for older males and is suggested by the analysis in Burdett et al. WAGE also affects the information arrival rate in the unemployment state. The effect is greater for blacks than it is for whites, which could indicate that high-wage blacks are at an employment advantage relative to low-wage blacks. Racial differences also exist in the magnitudes of the effect of the AFDC variable. In particular, AFDC payments tend to decrease the preference for employment for both races, but more so for blacks. Other public transfers have the same effect.

In sum, the results presented here are mixed. We cannot conclude that racial differences in labor force participation rate behavior are solely the result of differences in arrival rates, and we cannot conclude they are solely the result of differences in choice probabilities. Both forces seem to be at work.

Summary and Concluding Remarks

We have attempted to identify the impact that unemployment rates (a proxy for the level of job opportunities) have on individual workers' probabilities of making labor market transitions, controlling for individual differences in age, expected wages, nonlabor income, and education. The "reduced form" estimates presented here are fairly consistent with the results presented in chapter 3, suggesting that changes in job opportunities have their most significant effects on the E to U, N to U, U to E, and N to E transitions. Racial differences in these effects exist for the E to U, E to N, and N to U transitions, which contribute to the differential discouraged worker effect. "Structural estimates" suggest that the participation rate of blacks is lower because of significant racial differentials in the choice probability π_E and the information arrival rate α_N, and also because blacks receive on average lower wages and higher levels of public transfers.

6

Sources of Trends in Participation: Further Evidence from the Gross Flows

This chapter presents an analysis of the trends in labor force participation noted in chapter 2, in the context of the flow approach developed above. I begin by identifying the trends in transition rates that are the source of the trends in participation. I then examine some of the determinants of these transition rate trends, including the labor supply of women, and AFDC payments.

Identifying the Important Trends

I begin the analysis by estimating the trends in transition probabilities from the following regression equation:

$$\log(\lambda_{ij})_t = \beta_0 + \beta_1 t + \Gamma(\text{monthly dummies}) + u_t, \tag{6.1}$$

where u_t is an error term and the coefficient β_1 represents the rate of growth in λ_{ij}. The raw data is from the Current Population Survey's Gross Change Tabulations, for the 1972–82 time period. This analysis differs from that in chapter 3 only in that here I have excluded the proxy for aggregate demand, URATE. Because of serially correlated errors the estimates of the parameters are obtained using the Cochrane-Orcutt technique, assuming a first-order autoregressive process. The estimates of β_0 and β_1 are presented, by race, in table 6.1. The results of the analysis support the hypothesis that black and white transition rates have exhibited differential trends over the past decade, both in terms of the magnitudes and quite often the directions of the trends. To summarize the table, the probabilities of making the E to N and U to N transitions have been increasing for blacks, while the rates for whites have been decreasing. The probabilities of flows into the labor force, λ_{NE} and λ_{NU}, have been decreasing and increasing, respectively, for both races, though the magnitudes of the trends differ. Also, the N to E rate for whites does not seem to have a significant trend. Further, racial differences exist in the trends in the E to U and U to E rates. Whites have

Sources of Trends in Participation

Table 6.1. Regression Results: Equation (6.1)

Blacks

	EN	EU	UE	UN	NE	NU
Constant	2.4174*	1.8156*	2.8365*	3.4218*	1.7297*	1.9530*
b_1	.0013	-.0000	-.0044*	.0011*	-.0021*	.0012*
R^2	.6555	.2248	.4745	.5377	.7982	.7503
D.W.	2.006	1.929	2.018	2.002	1.978	1.978

Whites

	EN	EU	UE	UN	NE	NU
Constant	2.2253*	1.3736*	3.2992*	3.3324*	2.0907*	1.7445*
b_1	-.0009*	.0019*	-.0009	-.0010*	-.0005	.0021*
R^2	.9255	.5452	.5258	.6484	.9278	.8044
D.W.	2.0398	1.9770	2.2020	1.9606	1.9987	2.0645

*Significant at the 95 percent level of confidence.

become more likely to make the E to U transition, while blacks show no significant trend. The black trend coefficient for the U to E transition rate is negative, and almost 5 times the size of the white coefficient.

Using equation (3.11) from chapter 3, it is possible to measure the effects that these trends in transition rates have on the trends in participation rates noted in chapter 2, and to estimate the importance of the racial differences. Equation (3.11) expresses the participation rate as the following function of the transition probabilities:

$$r = \frac{U + E}{N + U + E},$$

$$= \frac{(\frac{a}{b}) + (\frac{c}{d})}{1 + (\frac{a}{b}) + (\frac{c}{d})}, \qquad (6.2)$$

where $a = ne + \left(\dfrac{ue \cdot nu}{ue + un}\right),$

$b = en + \left(\dfrac{un \cdot eu}{un + ue}\right),$

$c = nu + \left(\dfrac{eu \cdot ne}{eu + en}\right),$

and $d = un + \left(\dfrac{ue \cdot en}{eu + en}\right).$

I take the following approach: (1) Using the specification in (6.2), estimate the white and black participation rates implied by the average transition probabilities over the sample time period. (2) Estimate the black transition probabilities that would be implied if they had the white trends. (3) Estimate the black participation rates implied by the "new" transition probabilities. (4) Compare these participation rates with the ones generated in step (1).

For instance, let

$$r_t^B = r^B(\lambda_{EN}^B, \lambda_{EU}^B, \lambda_{UN}^B, \lambda_{UE}^B, \lambda_{NU}^B, \lambda_{NE}^B)$$

be the "actual" participation rate for blacks in period t, a function [equation (6.2)] of the "black transition rates," λ_{ij}^B.[1] Now define

$$\log(\lambda_{EN}^*) = \beta_0^B + \beta_1^W \cdot t$$

to be the log of the E to N transition rate for blacks, *if blacks had the white growth rate*, where β_0^B and β_1^W are the estimates of β_0 and β_1 from the black and white regression equations, respectively.

Let $r_t^B(en) = r^B(\lambda_{EN}^*, \lambda_{EU}^B, \ldots, \lambda_{NE}^B)$ be the participation rate that blacks would have if they had the E to N transition rate λ_{EN}^*. Any difference between r_t^B and $r_t^B(en)$ is therefore the result of the racial difference in the E to N transition probability growth rate, $\beta_1^B - \beta_1^W$. I estimate an $r_t^B(ij)$ for each transition probability, λ_{ij}.

The results of this analysis are presented in table 6.2. The variables used to "compare" the participation rates are the mean participation rate over the sample period and the estimated rate of growth in the rate. These are presented in columns (1) and (3). The rows are identified according to the transition rate that was changed to λ^* when calculating the participation rate. The participation rate presented in the first column of the first row is therefore the mean participation rate for blacks, assuming they had the *whites'* rate of growth in the E to N transition rate. The entry in the first row, third column is the *rate of growth* in the "new"

Table 6.2. Estimates of Mean Participation Rates and Growth Rates, under Alternative Growth Rate Assumptions

"Changed" Rate	Mean Participation Rate	Percent Difference from Actual Rate	Rate of Growth	Percent Difference from Actual Rate
EN	44.266	2.4840	-.0010	29.6187
EU	42.9725	-.5107	-.0015	-6.7181
UN	44.4084	2.8136	-.0008	39.5444
UE	43.1934	.0007	-.0014	.0000
NE	44.8131	3.7506	-.0006	55.3017
NU	43.6713	1.1071	-.0012	16.4853
All	47.7718	10.6005	-.0005	63.1514

participation rate [$r^B(en)$], the regression coefficient from a regression of log($r^B(en)$) on time. The last row of the table gives the variable values under the assumption that blacks had the white trends for *all* the transition rates.

In the second and fourth columns I present the percentage differences between the new participation rates and growth rates and the "actual" participation and growth rates. I use 43.19131 as the estimated mean of the actual participation rate, and −0.00139 as the approximate growth rate.

The results indicate that if all of the black transition rates had white trends, the average of the black participation rates over the past decade would have been more than 10 percent higher than its true value (row 7, column 2). In addition, the rate of decline in the participation rate would have been less than half the true rate. Three transition rates stand out in their effect: E to N (row 1), U to N (row 3), and N to E (row 5). The racial differential in the trend in the N to E transition rate is clearly the most important determinant of the racial differences in levels and trends in participation. If the transition rate for blacks had the same trend as the rate for whites the black participation rate would have been nearly 4 percent higher and would have declined at less than half the actual rate over the sample period.

The impacts of these differences on the *participation rate differential,* defined as the difference between the white and black participation rates, are presented in table 6.3. The impacts are substantial. Here I present the difference between the *averages* of the labor force participation rates for blacks and whites, under the assumptions that the respective transition rates exhibited the white trends.

Table 6.3. Estimates of Racial Differential in Participation, under Alternative Growth Rate Assumptions

"Changed" Rate	Estimated Racial Differential (Percentage Points)	Percent Decrease from Actual Differential
EN	17.5887	5.7492
EU	18.8822	-1.1821
UN	17.4463	6.5123
UE	18.6613	0.0016
NE	17.0416	8.6809
NU	18.1834	2.5625
All	14.0829	24.5354

Note: The actual mean participation rates for whites and blacks were 61.8547 and 43.1931 percent, respectively. The actual participation rate differential was therefore 18.6616 percentage points.

We see that the estimated racial differentials (column 1) range anywhere from 14.0829 to 18.8822 percentage points. The actual mean racial differential for the sample period was 18.6616 percentage points (61.8547 v. 43.1931), or 43.2 percent of the black participation rate. The entries in column 2 represent the percent difference between this actual rate and the estimated rate in column 1. The entries in the last row of the table therefore indicate that if black youth had the same trends in transition rates as white youth the mean racial differential would have been 14.0829 percentage points, a reduction of almost 25 percent. Elimination of the racial difference in the trend in the N to E transition rate alone would decrease the racial differential in participation by more than 8 percent (row 5, column 2).

Comments

The analysis in this section shows that significant racial differences in trends in transition rates exist, and that these differential trends contribute significantly to the differences in labor force participation that we have observed over the past decade. Differences in the E to N, N to E, and U to N rates stand out in their effects. The analysis is not complete, however, for I have not taken account of the relationships that may exist between the white and black transition rates. Depending in part on the degree to which white and black teenage labor markets

104   Sources of Trends in Participation

are segmented, a hypothetical increase in the N to E transition rate for blacks may necessarily correspond with a decrease in the N to E transition rate for whites, leading to a decrease in the white participation rate and a decrease in the racial differential greater than the decrease we estimated. Clearly, the extent of the bias depends on the extent to which the rate at which blacks and whites can expect to receive job offers are jointly determined.

We should keep in mind that the calculations above have been based on variations in transition probability *growth rates,* not levels. Certainly the racial differential in participation rates would exhibit even more drastic reduction if blacks had white transition rate levels.

Explaining the Trends

We put forth many variables in chapters 4 and 5 that affect the levels of transition probabilities, and hence possibly transition rate trends. In addition to the level of aggregate demand, these included expected wages and AFDC payments. In this section I present an analysis of the effects that similar variables have had on the trends. In addition, I analyze the effects of variables that directly affect the demand for teenage labor. In particular, I estimate the effects of the minimum wage, AFDC payments, the labor force activity of women, and the Youth Employment and Demonstration Projects Act, in addition to the level of aggregate demand.

The Data

The minimum wage variable (RELMIN) is defined to be the basic (federal) minimum wage, relative to the average hourly (nominal) wage for production and nonsupervisor workers. Note that the definition differs from the "effective minimum wage" or "Kaitz index" often used in other research in that no attempt has been made to control for the extent of coverage of the wage.[2] During the sample period studied here, however, the extent of coverage does not vary much, falling from 83.7 percent in 1974 to 83 and then rising to 83.8 percent by 1981.[3] I *have* conducted the analysis using the "effective minimum" definition in Hashimoto (1981), and using the data presented there have found no significant differences in the results.

The female "labor force activity" variable (WOMEN) is defined as the percent of the total labor force that is women. This variable is used over the labor force participation rate variable because it is less sensitive to cyclic variations in employment opportunities. The AFDC variable (AFDC) is the average monthly (nominal) AFDC payment received by AFDC families, relative to average hourly (nominal) wages. Also included in the analysis is a dummy variable to account for the Youth Employment and Demonstration Projects Act (YEDPA) noted above, and a proxy for the level of aggregate demand, the prime-age male unemployment rate (UPRIME).

Empirical Analysis

In table 6.4 I present estimates of the effects of these variables on levels of transition rates from the following regression equation:

$$\log(\lambda_{ij})_t = \beta_0 + \beta_1\log(\text{WOMEN})_t + \beta_2\log(\text{RELMIN})_t \qquad (6.3)$$
$$+ \beta_3\log(\text{AFDC})_t + \beta_4\log(\text{UPRIME})_t$$
$$+ \beta_5(\text{YEDPA})_t + \beta_6 t + \Gamma(\text{monthly dummies}) + u_t.$$

The results suggest that the most significant factors in the determination of the transition rates are the labor market activity of women and the level of AFDC payments, for both races. An increase in the labor supply of women is estimated to generate an increase in the U to N transition rate for male youth, though the effect is small and insignificant for whites. Increased female participation also has the effect of decreasing the N to E transition rate, for both races, and the U to E transition rate for blacks. To the extent that women's participation has risen over the past decade then it is likely a contributor to the positive trend in the U to N transition rate and the negative trend in the U to E transition rate for blacks, and the negative trend in the N to E transition rate (for both races) noted in table 6.1.

AFDC payments are important determinants of the U to E, U to N, and E to U transition rates for blacks and the U to E and E to N transition rates for whites. The effect has the predicted signs for most of the rates. AFDC payments seem to have the important effect of subsidizing search for blacks, decreasing the U to E and increasing the E to U and N to U rates. The minimum wage has its largest effect on the E to N and E to U transition rates, "marginally significant," but only for whites. Of course, as Gramlich (1976) and others have pointed out, we should not expect much of a minimum wage effect since the minimum wage relative to other wages has not changed much in the past twenty years.

As we have found, the most cyclically responsive transition rates are the U to E and N to E rates, for both races, and the E to U rate for whites. The Youth Employment and Demonstration Projects seem to have had significant effects on the U to E and N to U transition rates for blacks, and the E to N, U to E, and N to E rates for whites. The effect of this variable differs by race (in terms of its sign) for the U to N, N to E, and N to U transitions. This is probably simply because minority youth were those targeted by the program.

Racial differences exist in the effects of some of the other variables, also. The most important ones are in the effects of the WOMEN variable on the U to N, N to E, and U to E transitions, and the effect of the AFDC variable on the U to N and U to E transitions. A 1 percent increase in the WOMEN variable increases the U to N rate for blacks by 8.3 percent, compared to only .5 percent for whites. It decreases the N to E transition rate by more than 6 percent for blacks,

Table 6.4. Regression Results: Equation (6.3)

Blacks

	EN	EU	UE	UN	NE	NU
Constant	19.4236	-51.750	52.665*	-30.686*	18.147	-21.531
WOMEN	-4.267	11.403	-10.513**	8.319*	-6.425	4.557
AFDC	-.577	4.633**	-.503*	2.315*	1.661	2.233
RELMIN	-.383	.024	-.753	-.196	-.781	.125
UPRIME	-.147	-.248	-.248	-.009	-.320*	.110
YEDPA	-.171	.072	-.311*	.052	.246	.263*
TIME	.011	-.010	.008	-.918**	.015*	-.006
R^2	.663	.250	.590	.589	.852	.782
D.W.	2.012	1.923	1.789	2.028	1.993	1.990

Whites

	EN	EU	UE	UN	NE	NU
Constant	-1.850	-1.301	-9.677	6.139	17.449*	9.259
WOMEN	2.511	.539	1.860	.522	-4.307*	-2.444
AFDC	-1.294**	-.344	2.309*	-1.056	-.588	-.226
RELMIN	.408**	.560**	-.384	-.037	.121	.165
UPRIME	-.033	.259*	-.478*	-.038	-.221*	.247*
YEDPA	-.109*	.010	-.096**	-.013	-.094*	-.074
TIME	-.007*	-.002	.002	-.004	.008*	-.006
R^2	.937	.655	.814	.679	.959	.844
D.W.	1.951	2.002	2.186	1.981	1.973	2.001

Note: All coefficients are based on ARI assumption, except the *EN* and *UE* results which are from OLS regressions.

*Significant at the 95 percent level of confidence.
**Significant at the 90 percent level of confidence.

but by less than 5 percent for whites, though the effect is not statistically significant for blacks. It decreases the *U* to *E* transition rate by more than 10 percent for blacks, while it has a *positive* (but insignificant) effect for whites. The differential effect of the AFDC payments could be the result of a changing distribution (by race) of AFDC recipients, from black to whites. Partial evidence of such a shift lies in the fact that the proportion of AFDC recipients that is white had increased between 1975 and 1979, while the proportion that is black had fallen.

The effects of each of the variables on participation rates is straightforward, from equation (6.2). An increase in the proportion of women in the labor force leads to a decline in the labor force participation rate of male youth of both races. For whites this is due to an increase in the probability of making the transition from employment to out-of-the-labor-force, and a decrease in the probability of making the transition from out-of-the-labor-force to employment. For blacks, the increased supply of women contributes to their participation rate decline by significantly increasing their probability of making the unemployment to out-of-the-labor-force transition, and decreasing the probability of making the transition from unemployment to employment. The effect of AFDC payments on participation is, for blacks, to increase the probability of making the *U* to *N* transition which leads to a fall in the participation rate, to decrease the probability of making the *U* to *E* transition, and to increase the probability of making the *E* to *U* transition. The combined effect should be to decrease participation. For whites the effect of AFDC on participation rates is ambiguous.

The effect of the aggregate demand variable (UPRIME) on participation rates is seen through its effects on the *NE, NU, UE,* and *EU* variables for whites, and the *NE* variable for blacks. The "total" effect of an increase in the aggregate prime age male rate is to decrease participation rates, for both races.

The effects of the explanatory variables on transition rate *growth rates* can be estimated by "differencing" equation (6.4):

$$\log(\lambda_{ij})_t - \log(\lambda_{ij})_{t-1} = \alpha_0 + \alpha_1[\Delta\log(\text{WOMEN})] \quad (6.4)$$
$$+ \alpha_2[\Delta\log(\text{RELMIN})] + \alpha_3[\Delta\log(\text{AFDC})]$$
$$+ \alpha_4[\Delta\log(\text{UPRIME})]$$
$$+ \alpha\,[\Delta\log(\text{YEDPA})] + \Gamma(\text{monthly dummies}) + \varepsilon_t,$$

where "$\Delta\log(X)$" = $\log X_t - \log X_{t-1}$, and $\varepsilon_t = u_t - u_{t-1}$.

The coefficients are again estimated under the assumption that the error is first-order autoregressive.

The results are presented in table 6.5. One will note immediately that few of the estimated coefficients are significantly different from zero. This is probably

108   *Sources of Trends in Participation*

Table 6.5. Regression Results: Equation (6.4)

Blacks

	EN	EU	UE	UN	NE	NU
Constant	-.235**	-.399*	.255*	-.244	.192	.077
WOMEN	6.381	21.652	-.472	8.119	-9.320	-2.854
AFDC	-3.454	10.634**	1.363	2.464	4.354	3.628
RELMIN	.392	2.192	1.065	-.761	.307	-.706
UPRIME	.239	-.782	-.488	.204	-.187	-.209
YEDPA	-.147	-.229	-.447	.161	.104	.233
R^2	.704	.291	.479	.616	.753	.752
D.W.	2.064	2.195	2.217	2.443	2.363	2.437

Whites

	EN	EU	UE	UN	NE	NU
Constant	-.119*	-.158*	.208*	-.134*	-.145*	.131*
WOMEN	5.126	3.557	-.236	4.403	-14.371*	.790
AFDC	.351	3.910	4.782*	-.054	2.661	-.535
RELMIN	.533	.727	-.441	.286	.904	.844
UPRIME	-.267	.277	-.720*	.161	-.365	.185
YEDPA	.016	.244	-.034	.076	-.125	.047
R^2	.953	.560	.708	.745	.905	.852
D.W.	2.871	2.582	2.705	2.589	2.822	2.532

*Significant at the 95 percent level of confidence.
**Significant at the 90 percent level of confidence.

because the variables are very highly correlated with each other.[4] The estimates are unbiased, however,[5] and suggest again that the WOMEN and AFDC variables may be important contributors to the trends in transition rates already noted (table 6.1). The influx of women has had a positive impact on the rate of change in the E to N, E to U, and U to N transition rates, for both races, though the effects are larger for blacks. The variable is seen to decrease the U to E, N to E, and

N to *U* transition rates for blacks, and the *U* to *E* and *N* to *E* rates for whites. All of these effects would tend to decrease the rate of growth in participation rates.

Again, many racial differences exist in the effects of the AFDC variable. The signs are different for the *E* to *N*, *U* to *N*, and *N* to *U* transition rates. The magnitudes of the effects seem to differ for the *E* to *U* and *U* to *E* transition rates. Through its effects on the *E* to *U* and *U* to *N* rates, however, the AFDC variable has probably contributed significantly to the decreasing and increasing participation rates for black and white youth, respectively.

The directions of the effects of the UPRIME variable are almost all as would be expected, but the coefficients are not significantly different from zero except in the case of the *U* to *E* transitions for whites. Again, there is a problem of multicollinearity, so the results must be interpreted accordingly. Further research on this subject should use the "conditional omitted variable" or "weighted average" estimators suggested by Feldstein (1973) to adjust for this problem.

In conclusion, the analysis suggests that the increased labor supply of women over the past decade and increases in AFDC payments have contributed to the decline in the labor force participation rate of black male teenagers. It is evident from the "constants" in table 6.5, however, that significant trends in transition rates (and therefore participation rates) have been left unexplained.

7

Conclusions and Suggestions for Further Research

The goal of this study has been to theoretically and empirically examine the racial difference in the levels, trends, and cyclic rates of change of the labor force participation of male teenagers. The empirical analyses presented here have not "explained" all of the differences, but they have provided some evidence of their sources. The results suggest the following:

(1) The labor force participation rate is lower for blacks than for whites because blacks have higher probabilities of making transitions from employment to nonparticipation, employment to unemployment, and unemployment to nonparticipation, and lower probabilities of transitions from nonparticipation to employment and unemployment to employment. The higher flows for blacks from employment are the result of racial differences in the effects of AFDC payments, the worker's level of education, and the level of aggregate demand. This latter effect suggests the importance of differences in layoff or termination rates, and may suggest labor market discrimination. The lower flows for blacks *into* employment result from differences in the effects of AFDC and other transfer payments, and from some unobserved (or unmeasured) racial differences. These may include differences in the costs of search or participation in the "underground economy." In addition, transition rates into employment are lower for blacks because blacks have slightly lower information arrival rates in the unemployment and out-of-the-labor-force states.

(2) The labor force participation rate is more cyclically sensitive for blacks than for whites because of (a) racial differences in the cyclic variability of employment opportunities, and (b) racial differences in the cyclic responsiveness of transition rates from unemployment to nonparticipation, from nonparticipation to unemployment, and from nonparticipation to employment. The differences in the sensitivity of the transitions

from nonparticipation seem to result from a racial difference in the cyclic variability of the information arrival rate for "nonparticipant" workers. That is, blacks seem to receive fewer job offers per time period than do whites.

(3) The divergent trends in participation are the result of differential trends in the probability of making the employment to nonparticipation, unemployment to nonparticipation, and nonparticipation to employment transitions. The increased labor supply of women and AFDC payments have contributed to these trends.

In sum, there is support for the hypothesis that racial differences in participation behavior are the result of differences in "opportunities," in that differences in information arrival rates are important determinants of some of the transition rate differences. At the same time, there is some support for the hypothesis that the participation rate differences result from differences in "behavior," as is evidenced by the importance of the effects of AFDC payments.

There are many important variables that have been left out of this analysis, however, and many methodological questions that have not been addressed. In terms of excluded variables, differences in marital status and family size have been ignored, along with costs of job search. Further, school enrollment status has been ignored, as has the role of the demand for military personnel. Though it was argued that these variables do not explain the racial differences in participation in general, they certainly should contribute to individual variations in participation behavior and so should be included in the longitudinal data analysis. Data from the National Longitudinal Survey Youth Cohort, a survey of young men and women beginning in 1979, includes information on some of these variables. The analysis conducted here should be replicated using that data set. In terms of methodology, some extensions of the analysis that could be fruitful include attempting the Weibull analysis in chapter 5 using a specification that allows for nonmonotone duration effects, and using the ridge regression or weighted average approaches to the collinearity problems mentioned in chapter 6.

To summarize, the results of this study confirm the hypothesis that racial differences in employment opportunities and their variation over time contribute to the lower levels of labor force participation of black youth, to their greater cyclic sensitivity, and to their decline over the past decade. At the same time, a racial difference in the *response* to changes in employment opportunities also contributes to the cyclic and secular differences. I have attributed this difference to racial differences in the effects of AFDC and other public income transfer programs.

Notes

Chapter 2

1. Newman (1979).
2. This is only used as an example. It can be argued that the minimum wage does indeed have a direct effect on participation.
3. For a review of labor supply models, see Killingsworth (1983).
4. This model obviously ignores the intertemporal nature of the search decision. That is, it ignores the effects of today's decisions on *future* probabilities of finding employment. In more complex models, the effects of p may be indeterminant.
5. The most recent analysis of this hypothesis is in Mare and Winship (1983). Their paper deals with much broader questions, though, and provides only indirect evidence on this point.
6. In March of 1984, 43.1 percent of black families were headed by a female, compared to 12.6 percent of white families (U.S. Bureau of the Census, 1986).
7. Source: U.S. Census Bureau, *Current Population Reports*, Series P-20.
8. Classic papers that highlight these relationships include Mincer (1962) and Cain (1966). See also Tella (1966). For a dynamic analysis of household labor supply, see Lundberg (1981, 1985).
9. I refer here only to the expected change in participation resulting from a change in household income. As I will argue below, the increased supply of white women may very well have decreased the participation of black youth, but through its effect on employment opportunities.
10. Freeman (1983), page 3.
11. Andrisani (1977), page 309.
12. Page 315.
13. The contribution this has made to blacks' *employment* difficulties is discussed in the next section.
14. Source: U.S. Department of Labor, *Employment and Earnings* (1981, 1975).
15. The existence of internal labor markets is a characteristic often used to distinguish the "primary" from the "secondary" sectors of the labor market. See Doeringer and Piore (1971) and Gordon (1972).

114 Notes for Chapter 3

16. Flanagan (1978) makes this argument in explaining the fact that black workers have higher turnover rates than whites, regardless of age. Ragan and Smith (1981) make a similar argument regarding females.

17. Or, conversely, they pay for "better jobs" by receiving lower incomes.

18. A partial list of authors who refer to these relationships includes Bowers (1979);Iden (1976, 1980); Newman (1979); Young (1980); Congressional Budget Office (1976); U.S. Department of Labor (1980); and Freeman and Wise (1982). See particularly Anderson's article in the Congressional Budget Office report.

19. Bowers (1979), page 11.

20. Leon (1981), page 40.

21. Ragan (1977), page 131, in note 13.

22. Mincer (1966), page 99.

23. Osterman (1980), page 155.

24. Dayton (1981), page 324.

25. See Spence (1974) or Aigner and Cain (1977) for discussions of the problems this creates.

26. Employer preference is not the only possible source of discrimination, of course. See Phelps (1972) or Aigner and Cain (1977) for a discussion of the "statistical discrimination" that arises from basing individual hiring decisions on group or average productivities.

27. Blacks are less likely to enroll in college than whites are, however, and even more unlikely to graduate. But because we are concerned with the teenage age group, college enrollments are not very important. The source for all the statistics reported is the U.S. Bureau of the Census, *Current Population Reports*, Series P-20, No. 356.

28. Beaton (1975).

29. For a discussion of the meaning of cognitive test scores in general, see Jencks (1972). For discussions of the controversies surrounding the interpretations given to ability test scores, see the report of the National Research Council (1982).

30. A more complete discussion of the discrimination hypothesis follows.

31. See Adie and Chapman (1970); Adie (1971, 1973); Kosters and Welch (1972); Mincer (1976); Betsey and Dunson (1981); Iden (1980); Ragan (1977); Loury and Datcher (1981); and Ehrenberg and Marcus (1982). In contrast, see Brown, Gilroy, and Kohen (1983); or Meyer and Wise (1983) for estimates indicating no significant racial differences.

32. The minimum wage, for instance, has *fallen* relative to other wages over the past two decades. Even the extent of coverage of the minimum was constant over the decade of the seventies.

33. Gilman (1965) found that adult blacks were disproportionately concentrated in occupations which had the highest unemployment rates for *all* workers, and which had the greatest cyclical swings in employment.

34. Bowers (1979), p. 15.

Chapter 3

1. See Almon (1965).

2. See, for instance, Madalla (1977) or Judge et al. (1980), for discussions of this issue.

3. See U.S. Department of Labor (1982), Smith and Vanski (1980), or Abowd and Zellner (1983) for a discussion of these problems. They are not important here because they tend to bias point estimates of levels of transition rates, rather than changes over time.

4. After 1981, the gross change data has been tabulated for all "non-whites" together rather than for blacks alone, so that the more recent data is not useful in our analysis.

Chapter 4

1. Examples of "a change in the value of leisure" are the birth of a child, the unemployment of a spouse, or the receipt of some windfall profit. I will generally ignore the role of the value-of-leisure in this chapter, however, and concentrate instead on the role of wage (job) offers.

2. This section draws much from Mortensen and Neumann (1984).

3. This is the general specification. I will assume below that $\tilde{e}$ is in fact independent of the current value of e.

4. Recall that a layoff (a common form of unemployment) is the same as a zero wage offer, which is akin to a very low value of e_1.

5. See Mortensen and Neumann (1984).

6. For a complete discussion of the effects of wages on transition probabilities in the context of the model presented here, see Burdett et al. (1981).

7. For example, Johnson (1980).

8. Because the minimum wage creates an excess supply of labor at that wage, there is a range over the quantity of labor such that the supply curve of labor is perfectly elastic. Increases in the demand for labor therefore have no effects on the "equilibrium" wage.

9. This point was suggested to me by Professor Joel Mokyr.

Chapter 5

1. For an extensive derivation of the likelihood function used, see Williams (1984).

2. For a discussion of the censoring problem, see Flinn and Heckman, 1983; Kalbfleisch and Prentice, 1980; or Mortensen and Neumann, 1984.

3. For a more in-depth description of the data, see Kurz and Spiegelman (1972).

4. See Lundberg (1981) for a description of the methods used in constructing the data set.

5. There are nine structural vectors (three α's and six B's), and only six reduced form vectors (the δ's).

Chapter 6

1. The time index has been dropped from the transition rates for clarification purposes.

2. Examples of the "effective" minimum for years back to 1938 are presented in table 1 in Hashimoto (1981).

3. Hashimoto (1981), table 1.

4. For instance, Δ(WOMEN) and Δ(AFDC) have a correlation coefficient of more than .999.

5. At least, they are not biased as a result of the collinearity.

Bibliography

Abowd, John M., and Arnold Zellner. "Estimating Gross Labor Force Flows." Paper presented at the annual meeting of the American Statistical Association, August, 1983.
Adie, Douglas K. "'The Lag in Effect of Minimum Wages on Teenage Unemployment." *Proceedings of the Industrial Relations Research Association Meetings,* Winter, 1971.
_____. "Teenage Unemployment and Real Federal Minimum Wages." *Journal of Political Economy,* March/April, 1973.
_____, and Gene L. Chapin. "Teenage Unemployment Effects of Federal Minimum Wages." *Proceedings of the Industrial Relations Research Association Meetings,* Winter, 1970.
Aigner, Dennis J., and Glen G. Cain. "Statistical Theories of Discrimination in Labor Markets." *Industrial and Labor Relations Review,* January, 1977.
Alexis, Marcus, and Nancy DiTomaso. "Transportation, Race, and Employment: In Pursuit of the Elusive Triad." *Journal of Urban Affairs,* Spring, 1983.
Almon, S. "The Distributed Lag between Capital Appropriations and Net Expenditures." *Econometrica,* January, 1965.
Anderson, Bernard E. "Youth Employment Problems in the Inner City." In *The Teenage Employment Problem: What Are the Options?* Congressional Budget Office, October, 1976.
_____, and Isabel V. Sawhill. *Youth Unemployment and Public Policy.* Englewood Cliffs, N.J.: The American Assembly, 1980.
Anderson, Elijah. "Some Observations of Black Youth Employment." In B. Anderson and I. Sawhill, editors, *Youth Employment and Public Policy,* 1980.
Andrisani, Paul J. "Internal-External Attitudes, Personal Initiative, and the Labor Market Experience of White and Black Men." *Journal of Human Resources,* Summer, 1977.
Ashenfelter, Orley, and Albert Rees. *Discrimination in Labor Markets.* Princeton, N.J.: Princeton University Press. 1973.
Bartel, Ann. "Race Differences in Job Satisfaction: A Reappraisal." *Journal of Human Resources,* Spring, 1981.
Basmann, R., and G. Rhodes. *Advances in Econometrics.* Greenwich, Conn.: JAI Press, 1983.
Beaton, Albert E. "The Influence of Education and Ability on Salary and Attitudes." In F.T. Juster, ed., *Education, Income, and Human Behavior,* 1975.
Becker, Brian E., and Stephen M. Hills. "Teenage Unemployment: Some Evidence of Long-Run Effects on Wages." *Journal of Human Resources,* Summer, 1980.
_____. "Youth Attitudes and Adult Labor Market Activity." *Industrial Relations,* Winter, 1981.
Becker, Gary S. "A Theory of the Allocation of Time." *Economic Journal,* 1965.
Betsey, Charles L., and Bruce H. Dunson. "Federal Minimum Wage Laws and the Employment of Minority Youth." *American Economic Review,* May, 1981.

Borus, Michael E. "Willingness to Work Among Youth." *Journal of Human Resources,* Fall, 1982.
———. *Youth and the Labor Market.* Kalamazoo, Mich.: W. E. Upjohn Institute for Employment Research, 1984.
Bowen, William G., and T. Aldrich Finegan. "Labor Force Participation and Unemployment." In A. M. Ross, editor, *Employment Policy and the Labor Market,* 1965.
———. *The Economics of Labor Force Participation.* Princeton, N.J.: Princeton University Press. 1969.
Bowers, Norman. "Young and Marginal: An Overview of Youth Employment." *Monthly Labor Review,* October, 1979.
Brown, Charles. "Military Enlistments: What Can We Learn from Geographic Variations?" National Bureau of Economic Research Working Paper No. 1261, 1984.
———, Curtis Gilroy, and Andrew Kohen. "Time-Series Evidence of the Effect of the Minimum Wage on Youth Employment and Unemployment." NBER Working Paper No. 790, October, 1981.
Burdett, Kenneth, Nicholas M. Kiefer, Dale T. Mortensen, and George R. Neumann. "A Markov Model of Employment, Unemployment, and Labor Force Participation." Northwestern University, Discussion Paper No. 483, May, 1981.
Cain, Glen G. *Married Women in the Labor Force: An Economic Analysis.* Chicago: University of Chicago Press. 1966.
Clark, Kim B., and Lawrence Summers. "Demographic Differences in Cyclical Employment Variation." *Journal of Human Resources,* Winter, 1981.
Cogan, John F. "The Decline in Black Teenage Employment: 1950–1970." *American Economic Review,* September, 1982.
Cohen, Benjamin I. "Trends in Negro Employment Within Large Metropolitan Areas." *Public Policy,* Fall, 1971.
Congressional Budget Office. *The Teenage Unemployment Problem: What Are the Options?* Washington, D.C., 1976.
Crowley, Joan E. "Delinquency and Employment: Substitutions or Spurious Associations?" In M. E. Borus, editor, *Youth and the Labor Market,* 1984.
Datcher-Loury, Linda, and Glen C. Loury. "The Effects of Attitudes and Aspirations on the Labor Supply of Young Black Men." Paper presented at the National Bureau of Economic Research Conference on Inner City Black Youth Unemployment, Cambridge, Mass., August, 1983.
Dayton, Charles W. "The Young Person's Job Search: Insights from a Study." *Journal of Counselling Psychology,* July, 1981.
Dernberg, Thomas, and Kenneth Strand. "Hidden Unemployment 1953–1962: A Quantitative Analysis by Age and Sex." *American Economic Review,* March, 1966.
Doeringer, Peter, and Michael Piore. *Internal Labor Markets and Manpower Analysis.* Lexington, Mass.: Health, 1971.
Duncan, Beverly. "Dropouts and the Unemployed." *Journal of Political Economy,* April, 1965.
Duncan, Greg. "Labor Market Discrimination and Non-Pecuniary Work Rewards." In F. T. Juster, *The Distribution of Economic Well Being,* 1977.
Edwards, Linda N. "School Retention of Teenagers over the Business Cycle." *Journal of Human Resources,* Spring, 1976.
Ehrenberg, Ronald G. "The Demographic Structure of Unemployment Rates and Labor Market Transition Probabilities." Cornell University Monograph, July, 1979.
———, and Alan J. Marcus. "Minimum Wages and Teenagers' Enrollment-Employment Outcomes: A Multinomial Logit Model." *Journal of Human Resources,* Winter, 1982.
Eichengreen, Barry. "Casual Unemployment in Edwardian Britain: A New Look at Rowntree's York." Harvard University mimeograph, January, 1984.
Ellwood, David. "The Spatial Mismatch Hypothesis: Are There Teenage Jobs Missing in the Ghetto?" Paper presented at the National Bureau of Economic Research Conference on Inner City Black Youth Unemployment, Cambridge, Mass., August, 1983.

Feldstein, Martin S. "Multicollinearity and the Mean Square Error of Alternative Estimators." *Econometrica*, March, 1973.

Flanagan, Robert J. "Discrimination Theory, Labor Turnover, and Racial Unemployment Differentials." *Journal of Human Resources*, Spring, 1978.

Flinn, Christopher J., and James J. Heckman. "Models for the Analysis of Labor Force Dynamics." In R. Basmann and G. Rhodes, editors, *Advances in Econometrics*, 1982a.

——. "New Methods for Analyzing Structural Models of Labor Force Dynamics." *Journal of Econometrics*, 1982b.

——. "Are Unemployment and Out of the Labor Force Behaviorally Distinct Labor Force States?" *Journal of Labor Economics*, January, 1983.

Freeman, Richard B. "Teenage Unemployment: Can Reallocating Educational Resources Help?" In *The Teenage Unemployment Problem*, Congressional Budget Office, 1976.

——. "Black Economic Progress after 1964: Who Has Gained and Why?" National Bureau of Economic Research Working Paper No. 282, November, 1978.

——. "Have Black Economic Gains Post-1964 Been Permanent or Transitory?" National Bureau of Economic Research Working Paper No. 751, September, 1981.

——. "Who Escapes? The Relation of Church-going and Other Background Factors to the Socioeconomic Performance of Black Male Youth from Inner-City Poverty Tracts." Paper presented at the National Bureau of Economic Research Conference on Inner City Black Youth Unemployment, Cambridge, Mass., August, 1983.

——, and David A. Wise, editors. *The Youth Labor Market Problem: Its Nature, Causes, and Consequences.* Chicago: University of Chicago Press. 1982.

——, and Harry J. Holzer, editors. *The Black Youth Employment Crisis.* Chicago: University of Chicago Press, 1986.

Friedlander, Stanley L. *Unemployment in the Urban Core.* New York: Praeger. 1972.

Gilman, Harry J. "Economic Discrimination and Unemployment." *American Economic Review*, September, 1965.

Gordon, David. *Theories of Poverty and Unemployment.* Lexington, Mass.: Heath, 1972.

Gordon, Robert A., and Margaret S. Gordon. *Prosperity and Unemployment.* New York: Wiley. 1966.

Gordon, Robert J. "Discussion" of S. Marston, "Employment Instability and High Unemployment Rates," *Brookings Papers on Economic Activity*, 1:1976.

Gramlich, Edward M. "The Impact of Minimum Wages on Other Wages, Employment, and Family Income." *Brookings Papers on Economic Activity*, 2:1976.

Gustman, Alan L., and Thomas L. Steinmeier. "The Impact of Wages and Unemployment on Youth Enrollment and Labor Supply." *Review of Economics and Statistics*, November, 1981.

Hashimoto, Masanori. *Minimum Wages and On the Job Training.* Washington, D.C.: American Enterprise Institute for Public Policy Research. 1981.

Heckman, James J. "The Incidental Parameters Problem and the Problem of Initial Conditions in Estimating a Discrete Time-Discrete Data Stochastic Process." In C. F. Manski and D. McFadden, editors, *Structural Analysis of Discrete Data with Econometric Applications*, 1981.

Holzer, Harry J. "Black Youth Nonemployment: Duration and Job Search." In R. B. Freeman and H. J. Holzer, editors, *The Black Youth Employment Crisis*, 1986a.

——. "Reservation Wages and Their Labor Market Effects for Black and White Male Youth." *Journal of Human Resources*, Spring, 1986b.

——. "Informal Job Search and Black Youth Unemployment." NBER Working Paper No. 1860, March, 1986c.

Iden, George. "Policy Options for the Teenage Unemployment Problem." Congressional Budget Office, September, 1976.

——. "The Labor Force Experience of Black Youth: A Review." *Monthly Labor Review*, August, 1980.

Jencks, Christopher. *Inequality.* New York: Harper and Row, 1972.

Johnson, George. "The Theory of Labor Market Intervention." *Economica*, August, 1980.
Jovanovic, Boyan. "Job Matching and the Theory of Turnover." *Journal of Political Economy*, October, 1979.
Judge, George G., William E. Griffith, R. Carter Hill, and Tsoung-Chao Lee. *The Theory and Practice of Econometrics*. New York: Wiley. 1980.
Juster, F. Thomas. *Education, Income, and Human Behavior*. New York: McGraw-Hill. 1975.
———. *The Distribution of Economic Well Being*. Cambridge, Mass.: National Bureau of Economic Research. 1977.
Kaitz, Hyman B. "Analyzing the Lengths of Spells of Unemployment." *Monthly Labor Review*, November, 1970.
Kalbfleisch, John D., and Ross L. Prentice. *The Statistical Analysis of Failure Time Data*. New York: Wiley. 1980.
Kaun, David E. "Black-White Differentials in the Quality of Work." *Review of Black Political Economy*, Fall, 1975.
Kiefer, Nicholas M. "Evidence on the Role of Education in Labor Turnover." *Journal of Human Resources*, Summer, 1985.
Killingsworth, Mark R. *Labor Supply*. Cambridge: Cambridge University Press. 1983.
Kosters, Marvin, and Finis Welch. "The Effects of Minimum Wages by Race, Sex, and Age." In A. A. Pascal, editor, *Racial Discrimination in Economic Life*, 1972.
Kurz, M., and Robert G. Spiegelman. "The Design of the Seattle and Denver Income Maintenance Experiments." Research Memorandum 18, Stanford Research Institute, 1972.
Lazear, Edward. "Narrowing of Black-White Wage Differential is Illusory." *American Economic Review*, September, 1979.
Leon, Carol B. "The Employment-Participation Ratio: Its Value in Labor Force Analysis." *Monthly Labor Review*, February, 1981.
Lewis, H. Gregg. "Hours of Work and Hours of Leisure." *Proceedings of the Industrial Relations Research Association Meetings*, Winter, 1957.
———. *Aspects of Labor Economics*. Princeton, N.J.: Princeton University Press. 1963.
Long, Clarence. *The Labor Force Under Changing Income and Employment*. Cambridge, Mass.: National Bureau of Economic Research, 1958.
Loury, Glen, and Linda Datcher. "The Effect of Minimum Wage Legislation on the Distribution of Family Earnings among Blacks and Whites." In the *Report of the Minimum Wage Study Commission*, vol. 7, 1981.
Lundberg, Shelly J. "Unemployment and Household Labour Supply." Doctoral dissertation, Northwestern University, June, 1981.
———. "The Added Worker Effect." *Journal of Labor Economics*, January, 1985.
Madalla, G.S. *Econometrics*. New York: McGraw-Hill. 1977.
Manski, Charles F., and Daniel McFadden. *Structural Analysis of Discrete Data with Econometric Applications*. Cambridge, Mass,: MIT Press. 1981.
Mare, Robert D., and Christopher Winship. "Enrollment, Enlistment, and Employment, 1964-1981. Racial Socioeconomic Convergence and the Paradox of Black Youth Joblessness." Unpublished manuscript, April, 1983.
Marston, Stephen. "Employment Instability and High Unemployment Rates." *Brookings Papers on Economic Activity*, 1:1976.
Meyer, Robert H., and David A. Wise. "The Effects of the Minimum Wage on the Employment and Earnings of Youth." *Journal of Labor Economics*, January, 1983.
Mincer, Jacob. "Labor Force Participation of Married Women." In H. G. Lewis, editor, *Aspects of Labor Economics*, 1963.
———. "Labor Force Participation and Unemployment: A Review of Recent Evidence." In R. A. and M. S. Gordon, editors, *Prosperity and Unemployment*, 1966.
———. "Unemployment Effects of Minimum Wages." *Journal of Political Economy*, August, 1976.

Morse, Laurence C. "Increasing Unemployment and Changing Labor Market Expectations Among Black Male Teenagers." *American Economic Review*, May, 1981.

Mortensen, Dale T., and George R. Neumann. "Choice or Chance? A Structural Interpretation of Individual Labor Market Histories." In N. W. Nielson and G. R. Neumann, editors, *Labor Market Dynamics and Unemployment*, 1984.

National Research Council, Committee on Ability Testing. *Ability Testing: Uses, Consequences, and Controversies*. Washington, D.C.: National Academy Press, 1982.

Nielson, Niels W., and George R. Neumann. *Labor Market Dynamics and Unemployment*. Prague: Springer-Verlag. 1984.

Newman, Morris J. "The Labor Market Experience of Black Youth, 1954–78." *Monthly Labor Review*, October, 1979.

Olsen, Randall J., D. Alton Smith, and George Farkas. "Structural and Reduced-Form Models of Choice among Alternatives in Continuous Time: Youth Employment under a Guaranteed Jobs Program." *Econometrica*, March, 1986.

O'Neill, Dave M. "Racial Differentials in Teenage Unemployment: A Note on Trends." *Journal of Human Resources*, Spring, 1983.

Osterman, Paul. "Racial Differences in Male Youth Unemployment." In U.S. Department of Labor, *Conference Report on Youth Unemployment*, 1980.

Perry, George L. "Potential Output and Productivity." *Brookings Papers on Economic Activity*, 1:1977.

Phelps, Edward. "The Statistical Theory of Racism and Sexism." *American Economic Review*, September, 1972.

Plotnick, Robert. "Turnover in the AFDC Population: An Event History Analysis." *Journal of Human Resources*, Winter, 1983.

Ragan, J. F., Jr. "Minimum Wages and the Youth Labor Market." *Review of Economics and Statistics*, February, 1977.

———, and Sharon Smith. "The Impact of Differences in Turnover Rates on Male/Female Pay Differentials." *Journal of Human Resources*, 18:1981.

Rotter, J. B. "Generalized Expectations for Internal Versus External Control of Reinforcement." *Psychological Monographs*, No. 609, 1966.

Smith, Ralph E., and Jean E. Vanski. "The Volatility of the Teenage Labor Market: Labor Force Entry, Exit, and Unemployment Flows." In U.S. Department of Labor, *Conference Report on Youth Unemployment*, 1980.

Spence, Michael. "Job Market Signalling." *Quarterly Journal of Economics*, August, 1973.

Tella, Alfred. "The Relation of Labor Force to Employment." *Industrial and Labor Relations Review*, April, 1964.

———. "Labor Force Sensitivity to Employment by Age and Sex." *Industrial Relations*, February, 1965.

Tuma, Nancy Brandon, and Philip K. Robins. "A Dynamic Model of Employment Behavior: An Application to the Seattle and Denver Income Maintenance Experiments." *Econometrica*, May, 1980.

U.S. Department of Commerce, Bureau of the Census. *Current Population Reports*, Series P-20. Various issues, annual.

———. *Current Population Reports*, Series P-60. Various issues, annual.

———. *Statistical Abstract of the United States*. Various issues, annual.

U.S. Department of Education, National Center for Education Statistics. *Digest of Education Statistics*. Washington, D.C. 1986.

U.S. Department of Labor. *Conference Report on Youth Unemployment—Its Measurement and Meaning*. Youth Knowledge Development Report 2.1. Washington, D.C., May, 1980.

———, Bureau of Labor Statistics. "Gross Flow Data From the Current Population Survey, 1970–80." March, 1982.

———. *Employment and Earnings*. Various issues, monthly.

Bibliography

Viscusi, W. Kip. "Market Incentives for Criminal Behavior." Paper presented at the National Bureau of Economic Research Conference on Inner City Black Youth Unemployment, Cambridge, Mass., August, 1983.

Wachter, Michael L. "Comment on Gramlich." *Brookings Papers on Economic Activity,* 2:1976.

_____. "A Labor Supply Model for Secondary Workers." *Review of Economics and Statistics,* May, 1972.

_____. "Intermediate Swings in Labor Force Participation." *Brookings Papers on Economic Activity,* 2:1977.

_____, and Choongsoo Kim. "Time Series Changes in Youth Joblessness." In R. B. Freeman and D. A. Wise, editors, *The Youth Labor Market Problem,* 1982.

Welch, Finis. "Black-White Differences in Returns to Schooling." *American Economic Review,* December, 1973.

Weiner, Stuart. "A Survival Analysis of the Black-White Unemployment Rate Differential." Doctoral dissertation, Northwestern University, August, 1982.

Westcott, Diane N. "Youth in the Labor Force: An Area Study." *Monthly Labor Review,* July, 1976.

Williams, Donald R. "Racial Differences in the Labor Force Participation of Male Teenagers." Northwestern University, doctoral dissertation, August, 1984.

Young, Anne. "School and Work among Youth During the 1970's." *Monthly Labor Review,* September, 1980.

Index

Ability, native, 31
Acceptance sets, 68–69, 71–80
AFDC. *See* Aid to Families with Dependent Children
Aggregate demand, 2, 3, 4, 5, 12, 16, 20, 42, 62, 65, 66, 70, 71, 71–80, 81, 83, 87, 94, 99, 104, 111
Aid to Families with Dependent Children (AFDC), 3, 5, 19, 20, 30, 85, 87, 88, 89, 97, 99, 104, 105, 107, 108, 109, 111, 112. *See also* Income transfer payments
Alexis, Marcus, and DiTomaso, Nancy, 23–24
Ambition, 2
Anderson, Elijah, 24
Andrisani, Paul J., 21, 34
Arrival rate. *See* Information arrival rate
Attitudes. *See* Internal attitudes; External attitudes

Baby boom, 29, 30
Bartel, Ann, 26
Becker, Brian E., and Hills, Stephen M., 34–35
Becker, Gary S., 13
Betsey, Charles L., and Dunson, Bruce H., 36
Black power, 7, 24
Borus, Michael E., 24, 30
Bowen, William G., and Finegan, T. Aldrich, 16, 41, 42
Bowers, Norman, 22–23, 29, 37
Burdett, Kenneth, et al., 84, 88, 97
Bureau of Labor Statistics (U.S.), 4, 8
Business cycle, 1, 2, 12, 36, 38, 80

Cain, Glen G., 13
Carter administration, 8
Choice probability, 69, 70, 71, 72, 79, 80, 83, 94, 95, 97, 98
Clark, Kim B., and Summers, Lawrence, 36, 38, 41, 43, 44, 48, 58
Cogan, John F., 36
Cohen, Benjamin I., 37

Consumer Price Index, 19–20
Cost of search, 2, 4, 7, 12, 14, 22, 23, 28, 30, 39, 75, 79, 81, 87, 88, 111, 112
CPS. *See* Current Population Survey
Current Population Survey (CPS), 4, 5, 57, 99

Datcher-Loury, Linda, and Loury, Glen C., 21–22
Dayton, Charles W., 31
Denver Income Maintenance Experiment, 84. *See also* Seattle Income Maintenance Experiment
Dernberg, Thomas, and Strand, Kenneth, 29, 41, 42, 43, 44
Discouraged worker effect, 3, 4–5, 38, 41–62, 63–81, 84, 88, 97, 98; lagged, 47–53, 62
Discrimination, 6, 31, 35, 36, 38, 39, 65, 111
Duncan, Beverly, 17
Duncan, Greg, 25–26
Duration dependence, 84, 89

Education, 5, 13, 32–35, 37, 39, 83, 88, 111
Edwards, Linda N., 17
Ellwood, David, 37
Employment opportunities, 1, 2, 6, 19, 26, 37, 43, 56, 68, 71–80, 87, 89
Employment/population ratio, 29–31, 42, 43
Expected wage, 5, 13, 14, 19, 24, 26, 39, 75, 81, 83, 87, 97, 104
Experience, work, 31, 35, 37, 38, 39
Exponential function, 84
External attitudes, 21–22, 34–35, 37

Family responsibilities, 2, 7, 19
Feldstein, Martin S., 109
Female-headed households, 17, 21
Female labor force participation, 99, 104, 105, 107, 108, 109, 112. *See also* Women workers
Flanagan, Robert J., 30

Index

Flinn, Christopher J., and Heckman, James J., 84
Food stamps, 19, 20
Freeman, Richard, 20–21, 24
Friedlander, Stanley L., 37
Fringe benefits, 25, 26

Gordon, Robert J., 25
Gramblich, Edward M., 105
Gross flow approach, to labor market dynamics, 54–59
Gustman, Alan L., and Steinmeier, Thomas L., 16–17

Hashimato, Masanori, 104
Holzer, Harry J., 22, 26

Iden, George, 19, 29, 36
Income transfer payments, 3, 5, 14, 39, 44, 85, 87, 89, 97, 98, 111, 112
Increased expectations hypothesis, 26, 30
Information arrival rate, 64–66, 68, 69, 70–80, 81, 83, 94, 95, 97, 98, 111, 112
Internal attitudes, 21–22, 34–35, 37

Jencks, Christopher, 33
Job: satisfaction, 26, 39; search behavior, 30; search methods, 22, 31

Kaitz, Hyman B., 41, 42, 44
Kaun, David E., 26
Kiefer, Nicholas M., 84, 88

Labor: force, behavior, 1, 85; force, female participation, 99, 104, 105, 107, 108, 109, 112; market transition, 64; supply of, 29–31, 38
Lagged discouraged workers effect, 47–53, 62
Layoff, 111
Lazear, Edward, 25, 36
Leisure, preference for, 14, 28; value of, 2, 4, 14, 21, 63–71, 81, 87, 88
Lewis, H. Gregg, 13
Long, Clarence, 41
Lundburg, Shelly J., 84, 85

Mare, Robert D., and Winship, Christopher, 37
Medicaid, 20
Medicare, 20
Military enlistment, 7, 14, 17, 18, 36, 37, 39, 112
Mincer, Jacob, 13, 29, 36, 41, 42
Minimum wage, 5, 13, 24, 29, 30, 36, 80, 104, 105
Morse, Laurence C., 24, 30
Mortensen, Dale T., and Neumann, George R., 63, 83, 84, 88, 94, 95, 97

National Assessment of Education Progress, 32–33
National Longitudinal Survey (NLS), 6, 21–22, 24, 26, 112
Newman, Morris J., 7
NLS. *See* National Longitudinal Survey
Nonlabor income, 2, 14, 19, 20, 28, 30, 80, 83. *See also* Income transfer payments
Nonmarket activities, 2, 79, 97
Nonpecuniary rewards, 24, 25

Olsen, Randall J., et al., 94
On-the-job training, 36
Osterman, Paul, 22, 30, 36–37

Part-time employment, 17
Perry, George L., 41, 42
Plotnick, Robert, 19
Productivity, 29, 31, 35, 36, 38
Public transfer payments. *See* Income transfer payments

Quality of Employment Survey, 26

Ragan, J. F., Jr., 29, 36
Recession, 2, 20
Religion, 21
Rent subsidy program, 20
Reservation wage, 24, 71
Rotter, J. B., 21

School: enrollment, 7, 14–17, 18, 37, 39, 112; lunch program, 20
Schooling. *See* Education
Search cost, of employment. *See* Cost of search
Seattle Income Maintenance Experiments, 5, 83–98
Structural estimates, 98
Suburbanization of jobs, 37

Tastes, worker's, 2, 14
Tella, Alfred, 41, 42, 43, 44, 58
Transition: function, 83, 87, 95; labor market, 64; probability, 3, 5, 55, 57, 66, 100, 101; rate, 5, 55, 56, 57, 87, 88, 89, 94, 95, 99–104, 105
Tuma, Nancy Brandon, and Robins, Philip K., 84

Unemployment: compensation, 30, 44; rate, 4, 5, 17, 26, 28, 29, 30, 35, 36, 38, 41, 44, 47–48, 54, 56, 58, 59, 62, 68, 81, 83, 88, 89, 95, 97, 98, 104

Wachter, Michael L., 25; and Kim, Choongsoo, 25

Wage: growth, 25; offer, 30, 63–71, 80. *See also* Expected wage; Minimum wage; Wages
Wages, 2, 24, 25, 30, 89. *See also* Expected wage; Minimum wage; Wage
Wealth, effects of, on supply, 13, 14, 19, 25, 30, 80
Weibull function, 84, 112
Weiner, Stuart, 30, 84, 87
Welch, Finis, 32
Westcott, Diane N., 37

Willingness to work, 2, 30
Women workers, 20, 25. *See also* Female labor force participation
Work: attitudes, 39; ethnic, 2, 7, 21, 31, 97; experience, 31, 35, 37, 38, 39

YEDPA. *See* Youth Employment and Demonstration Projects Act
Youth Employment and Demonstration Projects Act (YEDPA), 8, 11, 12, 104, 105